cook's library

Fish &
Seafood

cook's library
Fish & Seafood

p

This is a Parragon Book
First published in 2003

Parragon
Queen Street House
4 Queen Street
Bath BA1 1HE, UK

ISBN: 0-75258-756-0

Printed in China

NOTE

This book uses metric and imperial measurements. Follow the same
units of measurement throughout; do not mix metric and imperial.
All spoon measurements are level: teaspoons are assumed to be 5 ml,
and tablespoons are assumed to be 15 ml. Unless otherwise stated,
milk is assumed to be full fat, eggs and individual vegetables such as
potatoes are medium, and pepper is freshly ground black pepper.

The times given for each recipe are an approximate guide only because the
preparation times may differ according to the techniques used by different
people and the cooking times may vary as a result of the type of oven used.
The preparation times include chilling and marinating times, where appropriate.

Recipes using raw or very lightly cooked eggs should be
avoided by infants, the elderly, pregnant women, convalescents,
and anyone suffering from an illness.

Contents

Introduction

Seafood rightly deserves its image as a healthy food. It is high in protein and has the added bonus that oily fish, such as mackerel and herring, is also high in polyunsaturated fatty acid (omega-3)– the fat that helps reduce cholesterol levels. White fish are a good source of minerals as well as being low in fat, especially if poached, steamed or lightly grilled. Although shellfish have been linked with high cholesterol, they are also low in saturated fats and are therefore fine eaten in moderation.

The sheer variety of fish and shellfish is staggering. If you decided to eat fish just once a week, you could go for a whole year without eating the same dish twice. Seafood is quick and easy to prepare, making it an attractive ingredient to the busy cook. Often sold ready to cook, fish can be prepared in minutes and most shellfish is sold already cooked, needing even less preparation.

Fish is also good value for money compared to meat, as there is much less waste. Making fish a regular part of your diet makes a lot of sense.

Buying Fish and Shellfish

Wherever you are shopping for fish, at your local trusted fishmonger or supermarket, the guidelines are the same:

* The eyes of the fish should be clear, bright and moist. Fish with dull, grey or cloudy eyes should be avoided.

* The gills of the fish should be bright red or pink, not dull and grey.

* The fish should smell of the sea and nothing else.

* If you press the fish lightly with your thumb, the flesh should spring back, leaving little or no imprint.

* The shells of hinged shellfish, such as oysters, mussels and clams, should be tightly closed prior to cooking. If they are slightly open, tap them sharply. If they do not close, discard them.

* Cooked shellfish should smell fresh, with no hint of ammonia. If available, check the use-by date.

Storing

As you never know how long ago the fish was caught, especially in a supermarket, it is best to buy fish and cook it on the same day. Unfortunately, modern refrigerators are not an ideal place to store fish as they tend to have a temperature of about 5°C/41°F and fish is best kept at 0°C/32°F. If you have to keep fish, don't keep it for more than one or two days. Put the fish into a large plastic container and scatter over some ice. Cover with clingfilm and keep in the coldest part of the refrigerator.

Firmer fleshed fish, such as turbot, Dover sole and monkfish, freeze better than less firm-fleshed fish like sea bass, lemon sole and plaice but all will deteriorate over a relatively short period. Oily fish is the least successful when frozen. However, if you have to keep your fish for more than a day or two, then freezing is the best option. Ensure that you thaw fish thoroughly and slowly before cooking.

Preparation

The amount of preparation your fish needs depends on where you buy it. Supermarkets may have a wet fish counter with a trained fishmonger on hand while others sell their fish vacuum-packed. Many fish are sold already scaled and gutted, and are often available either whole or filleted. It is usually cheaper, however, to buy a whole fish and prepare it yourself. A fishmonger will usually do this job for you as part of the price of a whole fish. However, it is not difficult to do yourself and only takes some practice.

Equipment

Although, in general, you don't need a great deal of specialist equipment, there are a few items you might consider if you plan on cooking a lot of fish. If, for example, you are planning on poaching whole fish, then a wise investment would be a fish kettle. This is an oblong stainless steel pan with a lifter and lid. They usually come in several sizes.

A wok or large, heavy-based frying pan is useful for frying and stir-frying. If you like to steam fish you might consider buying a double boiler, bamboo steamer or electric steamer. A thermometer is useful for deep-frying as is a deep-frying basket and large pan. If you intend cleaning your own fish, a good filleting knife is a must. Tweezers are also useful for removing small bones.

Cooking Methods

Different fish suit different cooking methods but, as a general rule, poaching, steaming and stewing tend to produce moister results than grilling, baking or barbecuing. Drying out can be minimised, however, if the latter three methods are used at sufficiently high temperatures to reduce moisture loss by cooking the fish very quickly.

Poaching

The fish is immersed in a poaching liquid, which might be a court-bouillon, fish stock, milk, beer or cider. Bring the liquid to the boil and as soon as it boils, remove the pan from the heat and leave the fish to finish cooking in the residual heat. This method helps to prevent overcooking and is also excellent if you want to serve the fish cold.

Steaming

Both fish and shellfish benefit from being steamed. Again, a flavoured liquid can be used for the steaming, which will impart some of its flavour to the fish as it is being cooked. This method is especially good for keeping the fish moist and the flavour delicate. Steaming can be done in a fish kettle, a double boiler or a steamer inserted over a pan of boiling water.

Stewing

Either whole fish or smaller pieces can be cooked in liquid along with other ingredients, such as vegetables, as a stew. The fish flavours the liquid as it cooks, giving a distinctive flavour.

Grilling

This is one of the quickest and easiest cooking methods for fish. Cook either whole fish, steaks or fillets. Shellfish can also be grilled, but may need halving lengthways first. Whatever you are cooking, ensure that the grill is on its highest setting and that the fish is cooked as close to the heat source as possible. A barbecue is also very useful for grilling fish. Brush the fish with butter, oil or a marinade before and during cooking to ensure that the flesh remains moist.

Baking and Roasting

This covers all methods of cooking in the oven, including open roasting, casseroling or cooking en papillote. This is a good method to choose for entertaining because, once the dish is in the oven, you are free to attend to other things.

Deep-frying

The fish is coated in batter, flour or breadcrumbs and deep-fried in oil. You need a large, heavy-based saucepan or a deep-fat fryer. Large pieces of fish in batter are best cooked at a lower temperature of 180°C/350°F, which allows the fish to cook without burning the batter. Smaller pieces of fish, like goujons in breadcrumbs, should be cooked at a higher temperature of 190°C/375°F. Drain deep-fried items well on kitchen paper to ensure that they remain crisp.

Shallow or Pan-frying

This is a quick method for cooking fish and shellfish and can take as little as 3–4 minutes. A shallow layer of oil or butter and oil is heated in a frying pan, the fish added and cooked until just tender and lightly browned. A large, heavy-based, non-stick frying pan is an essential piece of equipment.

The argument for increasing the amount of fish and seafood in our diets is compelling. Fish and shellfish can provide variety, versatility, creativity and luxury as well as being much more healthy than meat. Why not give it a try?

Basic Recipes

These recipes form the basis of several of the dishes contained throughout this book. Many of these basic recipes can be made in advance and stored in the refrigerator until required.

Fresh Chicken Stock

MAKES
1.7 LITRES/3 PINTS

1 kg/2 lb 4 oz chicken, skinned
2 celery sticks, chopped
1 onion, sliced
2 carrots, chopped
1 garlic clove
few sprigs of fresh parsley
2 litres/3½ pints water
salt and pepper

1 Place all the ingredients in a large saucepan and bring to the boil over a medium heat.

2 Skim away any surface scum with a large flat spoon. Reduce the heat to a gentle simmer, partially cover, and cook for 2 hours. Leave to cool.

3 Line a sieve with clean muslin and place it over a large jug or bowl. Pour the stock through the sieve. The cooked chicken can be used in another recipe. Discard the other solids. Cover the stock and chill.

4 Skim away any surface fat before using. Store in the refrigerator for up to 3 days or freeze in small batches until required.

Fresh Vegetable Stock

MAKES
1.7 LITRES/3 PINTS

1 large onion, sliced
1 large carrot, diced
1 celery stick, chopped
2 garlic cloves
1 dried bay leaf
few sprigs of fresh parsley
pinch of grated nutmeg
2 litres/3½ pints water
salt and pepper

1 Place all the ingredients in a large saucepan and bring to the boil over a medium heat.

2 Skim away any surface scum with a large flat spoon. Reduce the heat to a simmer, partially cover, and cook for 45 minutes. Leave to cool.

3 Line a sieve with clean muslin and place it over a large jug or bowl. Pour the stock through the sieve. Discard the solids.

4 Cover the stock and store in the refrigerator for up to 3 days or freeze in small batches.

Fresh Fish Stock

MAKES
1.7 LITRES/3 PINTS

1 kg/2 lb 4 oz white fish bones, heads and scraps
1 large onion, chopped
2 carrots, chopped
2 celery sticks, chopped
½ tsp black peppercorns
½ tsp grated lemon rind
few sprigs of fresh parsley
2 litres/3½ pints water
salt and pepper

1 Rinse the fish trimmings in cold water and place in a large saucepan with the other ingredients. Bring to the boil over a medium heat.

2 Skim away any surface scum with a large flat spoon.

3 Reduce the heat to a gentle simmer and cook, partially covered, for 30 minutes. Leave to cool.

4 Line a sieve with clean muslin and place it over a large jug or bowl. Pour the stock through the sieve. Discard the solids. Cover the stock and store in the refrigerator for up to 3 days or freeze in small batches.

Fresh Beef Stock

MAKES
1.7 LITRES/3 PINTS

about 1 kg/2 lb 4 oz bones from a cooked
    joint or raw chopped beef
2 onions, studded with 6 cloves, or sliced
    or roughly chopped
2 carrots, sliced
1 leek, sliced
1–2 celery sticks, sliced
1 Bouquet Garni
about 2.2 litres/4 pints water

1 Use chopped marrow bones with
a few strips of shin of beef, if
possible. Put into a roasting tin
and cook in a preheated oven,
230°C/450°F/Gas Mark 8, for about
40–50 minutes or until browned.

2 Transfer to a large saucepan with
the other ingredients. Bring to
the boil over a medium heat.
Remove any scum from the
surface with a large flat spoon.

3 Cover and simmer gently for
3–4 hours. Strain the stock and
leave to cool. Remove any fat
from the surface and chill. If
stored for more than 24 hours the
stock must be boiled every day,
cooled quickly and chilled again.

4 The stock may be frozen for up to
2 months. Pour it in a large
polythene bag and seal, leaving at
least 2.5-cm/1-inch of headspace
to allow for expansion.

Chinese Stock

MAKES
2.5 LITRES/4¹/₂ PINTS

750 g/1 lb 10 oz chicken pieces, trimmed
    and chopped
750 g/1 lb 10 oz pork spare ribs
3.7 litres/6 pints cold water
3–4 pieces of fresh root ginger, chopped
3–4 spring onions, each tied into
    a knot
3–4 tbsp Chinese rice wine or dry sherry

1 Place the chicken and pork in a
large saucepan with the water.
Add the ginger and spring onions.

2 Bring to the boil over a medium
heat. Remove any surface scum
with a large flat spoon. Reduce
the heat and simmer, uncovered,
for at least 2–3 hours.

3 Strain the stock, discarding the
chicken, pork, ginger and spring
onions. Add the Chinese rice wine
and return to the boil, then
reduce the heat and simmer for
2–3 minutes. Leave to cool.

4 Store the stock when cool in the
refrigerator. It will keep for up to
4–5 days. Alternatively, it can be
frozen in small batches and
thawed as required.

Cornflour Paste

Mix 1 part cornflour with about
1.5 parts of cold water. Stir until
smooth. The paste can be used to
thicken sauces.

Fresh Bouquet Garni

1 fresh or dried bay leaf
few sprigs of fresh parsley
few sprigs of fresh thyme

Tie the herbs together with a length
of string or cotton.

Dried Bouquet Garni

1 dried bay leaf
good pinch of dried mixed herbs or any
    one herb
good pinch of dried parsley
8–10 black peppercorns
2–4 cloves
1 garlic clove, optional

Put all the ingredients into a small
square of muslin and tie with string
or cotton, leaving a long tail so it can
be tied to the handle of the pan for
easy removal.

How to Use This Book

Each recipe contains a wealth of useful information, including a breakdown of nutritional quantities, preparation and cooking times, and level of difficulty. All of this information is explained in detail below.

A full-colour photograph of the finished dish.

28

FISH & SEAFOOD

These crisp, golden-fried little mouthfuls are packed with flavour and served with a hot-and-sweet soy dip – perfect to stimulate appetites at the start of a meal, or as a tasty snack.

Tiger Prawn Rolls

SERVES 4

dip
1 small red bird's-eye chilli, deseeded
1 tsp clear honey
4 tbsp soy sauce

rolls
2 tbsp fresh coriander leaves
1 garlic clove
1½ tsp Thai red curry paste
16 wonton wrappers
1 egg white, beaten lightly
16 raw tiger prawns, peeled with tails intact
600 ml/1 pint sunflower oil, for deep-frying
whole fresh red chillies, to garnish

1 To make the dip, finely chop the chilli, then mix with the honey and soy and stir well. Reserve until required.

2 To make the prawn rolls, finely chop the coriander and garlic, and mix with the red curry paste.

3 Brush each wonton wrapper with egg white and place a small dab of the coriander mixture in the centre. Place a prawn on top.

4 Fold the wonton wrapper over, enclosing the prawn and leaving the tail exposed. Repeat with the other prawns.

5 Fill a deep-fat fryer or deep saucepan about one-third full with sunflower oil and heat to 180°C/350°F, or until a cube of bread turns brown in 30 seconds. Add the prawn rolls in small batches and fry for 1–2 minutes each until golden brown and crisp. Drain on kitchen paper and transfer to a large serving plate. Garnish with fresh chillies and serve with the dip. Give each guest a small bowl filled with hot water and a lemon slice, so that they can wash their fingers afterwards.

NUTRITION
Calories 175; Sugars 2 g; Protein 10 g; Carbohydrate 7 g; Fat 12 g; Saturates 1 g

⭐⭐   easy
🕐   10 mins
🕐   20 mins

COOK'S TIP

If you prefer, replace the wonton wrappers with filo pastry – use a long strip of pastry, place the paste and a prawn on one end, brush with egg white and wrap the pastry around the prawns to enclose, then fry.

The ingredients for each recipe are listed in the order that they are used.

The nutritional information provided for each recipe is per serving or per portion. Optional ingredients, variations or serving suggestions have not been included in the calculations.

The method is clearly explained with step-by-step instructions that are easy to follow.

Cook's tips provide useful information regarding ingredients or cooking techniques.

⭐ The number of stars represents the difficulty of each recipe, ranging from very easy (1 star) to challenging (4 stars).

🕐 This amount of time represents the preparation of ingredients, including cooling, chilling and soaking times.

🕐 This represents the cooking time.

Snacks *and* Starters

The dishes in this chapter are designed either to whet the appetite for the main course to come, without being filling, or as nibbles to serve with drinks. Fish and seafood make excellent starters as they are full of flavour and can be turned into a variety of delicious dishes.

Fish cooks quickly, making it ideal for entertaining. Many of the dishes in this chapter can be prepared in advance and served cold, such as the Anchovy Bites, the Smoked Mackerel Pâté and the Lime & Basil Cured Salmon.

There is a wide selection to suit all tastes, for example the Thai Crab Omelette, Potted Shrimps and Maryland Crab Cakes with a basil and tomato dressing, with lots of salad ideas, including the Smoked Haddock Salad and the Bruschetta with Anchoiade, accompanied by a mixed salad of tomatoes and mozzarella cheese.

These delicious pastry pinwheels are perfect for serving with drinks before dinner. If you prefer, use a ready-made anchovy paste, such as Gentleman's Relish, to save time.

Anchovy Bites

MAKES 30

175 g/6 oz plain flour, plus extra for dusting
85 g/3 oz butter, cut into small pieces
4 tbsp freshly grated Parmesan cheese
2–3 tbsp cold water
3 tbsp Dijon mustard
salt and pepper

anchoiade

115 g/4 oz canned anchovy fillets
 in olive oil, drained
100 ml/3½ fl oz milk
2 garlic cloves, chopped roughly
1 tbsp chopped fresh flat-leaved parsley
1 tbsp chopped fresh basil
1 tbsp lemon juice
25 g/1 oz blanched almonds, toasted and
 roughly chopped
4 tbsp olive oil

NUTRITION
Calories 77; Sugars 0.5 g; Protein 2 g;
Carbohydrate 5 g; Fat 5 g; Saturates 2 g

easy

1 hr

20 mins

1 To make the pastry, sift the flour into a large bowl. Add the butter and rub it in with your fingertips until the mixture resembles breadcrumbs. Stir in half the Parmesan cheese and salt. Add enough cold water to form a firm dough. Knead briefly, wrap in clingfilm and leave to chill for 30 minutes.

2 Meanwhile, make the anchoiade. Put the drained anchovies into a small bowl and pour over the milk to cover. Leave to soak for 10 minutes. Drain the anchovies and pat dry on kitchen paper. Discard the milk.

3 Roughly chop the anchovies and put into a food processor or blender with the garlic, parsley, basil, lemon juice, almonds and 2 tablespoons of the olive oil. Process until smooth, then transfer to a bowl and stir in the remaining olive oil and pepper to taste. Reserve.

4 Remove the pastry from the refrigerator and roll out very thinly on a lightly floured work surface to a rectangle measuring 50 x 38 cm/20 x 15 inches. Spread thinly with 2 tablespoons of the anchoiade and the Dijon mustard. Sprinkle over the remaining Parmesan cheese and some pepper.

5 Beginning from a long edge, roll up tightly, then slice the roll crossways into 1-cm/½-inch thick slices. Arrange cut side up and well spaced on a non-stick baking sheet.

6 Cook in a preheated oven, 200°C/400°F/Gas Mark 6, for 20 minutes until golden. Leave to cool on a wire rack.

This colourful salad is full of flavour and textures. Here, mixed cherry tomatoes and beefsteak or plum tomatoes are used, but the salad will work well with whatever ripe tomatoes are available.

Bruschetta *with* Anchoiade

1 Slice the mozzarella cheese into thick slices and reserve. Halve the cherry tomatoes and thickly slice the plum or beefsteak tomatoes.

2 To make the dressing, whisk the olive oil, balsamic vinegar and salt and pepper together in a small bowl.

3 Toast the bread on both sides, then rub one side with the garlic clove. Drizzle with a little olive oil. Spread the anchoiade on the toasts.

4 To assemble the salad, arrange the sliced tomatoes on each of 4 serving plates and scatter with some of the cherry tomatoes.

5 Top the toasts with the mozzarella cheese slices and 2–3 halved cherry tomatoes. Cook under a preheated medium–hot grill for 3–4 minutes until softened. Put 2 slices of toast on the salad plates and drizzle over the dressing. Scatter with basil leaves and pepper, then serve immediately.

SERVES 4

300 g/10½ oz mozzarella cheese
115 g/4 oz orange cherry tomatoes
115 g/4 oz red cherry tomatoes
2 ripe plum or red beefsteak tomatoes
2 ripe orange or yellow beefsteak tomatoes
4 tbsp extra virgin olive oil, plus extra for drizzling
1 tbsp balsamic vinegar
8 thick slices ciabatta or other rustic country bread
1 garlic clove
4 tbsp anchoiade (see page 20)
handful of fresh basil leaves
salt and pepper

NUTRITION
Calories *583*; Sugars *5 g*; Protein *28 g*;
Carbohydrate *39 g*; Fat *35 g*; Saturates *12 g*

 easy

 10 mins

 4 mins

🍳 **COOK'S TIP**

Look for Italian mozzarella cheese made from buffalo milk for this recipe for a real authentic taste of Italy.

Translated literally, *bagna cauda* means 'hot bath'. This is a typical dish from Piedmont in Italy, where it is always eaten by large groups gathered around the table.

Bagna Cauda *with* Crudités

SERVES 8

1 yellow pepper
3 celery sticks
2 carrots, peeled
½ cauliflower
115 g/4 oz mushrooms
1 fennel bulb
1 bunch of spring onions
2 beetroot, cooked and peeled
8 radishes
225 g/8 oz boiled new potatoes
225 ml/8 fl oz olive oil (not extra virgin)
5 garlic cloves, crushed
50 g/1¾ oz canned anchovy fillets in oil, drained and chopped
115 g/4 oz butter
shredded spring onion curls, to garnish

1 Prepare the vegetables. Deseed and slice the pepper thickly. Cut the celery into 7.5-cm/3-inch lengths. Cut the carrots into batons. Score the tops of the mushrooms. Separate the cauliflower into florets. Cut the fennel in half lengthways, then cut each half into 4 lengthways. Trim the spring onions. Cut the beetroot into eighths. Trim the radishes and cut the potatoes in half, if large. Arrange the prepared vegetables on a large serving platter.

2 Heat the olive oil very gently in a saucepan over a low heat. Add the garlic and anchovies and cook very gently, stirring constantly, until the anchovies have dissolved. Take care not to brown or burn the garlic.

3 Add the butter and as soon as it has melted, transfer to a small serving dish. Garnish with a few spring onion curls and serve immediately with the selection of prepared crudités.

NUTRITION

Calories *421*; Sugars *6 g*; Protein *7 g*; Carbohydrate *25 g*; Fat *33 g*; Saturates *11 g*

easy

20–30 mins

5–10 mins

 COOK'S TIP

If you have one, a fondue set is perfect for serving this dish as the sauce can be kept hot at the table.

In Spain, giant garlic prawns are cooked in small half-glazed earthenware dishes called *cazuelas*. The prawns arrive at your table sizzling.

Giant Garlic Prawns

1 Heat the olive oil in a large, heavy-based frying pan over a low heat. Add the garlic and chillies and cook, stirring occasionally, for 1–2 minutes until softened, but not coloured.

2 Add the prawns and stir-fry for 2–3 minutes until heated through and coated in the oil and garlic mixture.

3 Remove the pan from the heat and add the chopped parsley, stirring well to mix. Season to taste with salt and pepper.

4 Transfer the prawns and garlic-flavoured oil to 4 warmed serving dishes and garnish with lemon wedges. Serve immediately with lots of crusty bread.

SERVES 4

125 ml/4 fl oz olive oil
4 garlic cloves, chopped finely
2 hot fresh red chillies, deseeded and finely chopped
450 g/1 lb cooked king prawns
2 tbsp chopped fresh flat-leaved parsley
salt and pepper
lemon wedges, to garnish
crusty bread, to serve

NUTRITION
Calories *385*; Sugars *0 g*; Protein *26 g*; Carbohydrate *1 g*; Fat *31 g*; Saturates *5 g*

 easy

5 mins

5–8 mins

 COOK'S TIP

If using raw prawns, cook them as above, but cook for 5–6 minutes so that the prawns are cooked through and turn bright pink. If using frozen prawns, make sure they are thoroughly thawed before cooking.

These delicious little spring rolls are perfect as part of a selection of canapés. Serve with a selection of dips, as suggested in the recipe.

Mini Prawn Spring Rolls

SERVES 4

50 g/1³/₄ oz dried rice vermicelli
1 carrot, cut into matchsticks
50 g/1³/₄ oz mangetouts, shredded thinly lengthways
3 spring onions, chopped finely
100 g/3¹/₂ oz cooked peeled prawns
2 garlic cloves, crushed
1 tsp sesame oil
2 tbsp light soy sauce
1 tsp chilli sauce
200 g/7 oz filo pastry, cut into 15-cm/6-inch squares
1 egg white, beaten
600 ml/1 pint vegetable oil, for deep-frying
dark soy sauce, sweet chilli sauce or sweet and sour dipping sauce (see page 65) for dipping

NUTRITION
Calories *355*; Sugars *3 g*; Protein *13 g*; Carbohydrate *44 g*; Fat *14 g*; Saturates *2 g*

easy

10 mins

20 mins

1 Cook the rice vermicelli according to the packet instructions. Drain thoroughly. Roughly chop and reserve. Bring a saucepan of lightly salted water to the boil over a medium heat. Add the carrot and mangetouts and blanch for 1 minute. Drain and refresh under cold running water. Drain again and pat dry on kitchen paper. Mix with the noodles and add the spring onions, prawns, garlic, sesame oil, soy sauce and chilli sauce. Reserve.

2 Fold the filo pastry squares in half diagonally to form triangles. Lay a triangle on the work surface, with the fold facing you, and place a spoonful of the mixture in the centre. Roll over the wrapper to enclose the filling, then bring over the corners to enclose the ends of the roll. Brush the point of the spring roll furthest from you with a little beaten egg white and continue rolling to seal. Continue with the remaining filo triangles to make about 30 spring rolls.

3 Fill a deep-fat fryer or deep saucepan about one-third full with vegetable oil and heat to 190°C/375°F, or until a cube of bread browns in 30 seconds. Add the spring rolls, 4 or 5 at a time, and fry for 1–2 minutes or until golden and crisp. Drain on kitchen paper. Keep warm while you cook the remaining spring rolls.

4 Serve with soy sauce, sweet chilli sauce or sweet and sour sauce for dipping.

It is well worth seeking a supplier of Thai ingredients, such as lemon grass and lime leaves, as they add such distinctive flavours for which there are no real substitutes.

Prawn Satay

1 Slit the prawns down their backs and remove the black vein, if any. Reserve. Mix the marinade ingredients together and add the prawns. Mix well, cover and leave to marinate in the refrigerator for at least 8 hours or overnight.

2 To make the peanut sauce, heat the vegetable oil in a large frying pan until very hot. Add the garlic and fry until just beginning to colour. Add the curry paste and mix well, cooking for a further 30 seconds. Add the coconut milk, stock, sugar, salt and lemon juice and stir well. Boil for 1–2 minutes, stirring constantly. Add the peanuts and breadcrumbs and mix well. Pour the sauce into a bowl and reserve.

3 Using 4 metal skewers, thread 3 prawns on to each. Cook under a preheated hot grill or transfer to a lit barbecue and cook over hot coals for 3–4 minutes on each side until just cooked through. Transfer the prawns to a large serving plate, garnish with lime wedges and serve immediately with the peanut sauce, garnished with a lime wedge and a few whole peanuts.

SERVES 4

12 raw king prawns, peeled
lime wedges, to garnish

marinade
1 tsp ground coriander
1 tsp ground cumin
2 tbsp light soy sauce
4 tbsp vegetable oil
1 tbsp curry powder
1 tbsp ground turmeric
120 ml/4 fl oz coconut milk
3 tbsp sugar

peanut sauce
2 tbsp vegetable oil
3 garlic cloves, crushed
1 tbsp red curry paste (see page 74)
125 ml/4 fl oz coconut milk
225 ml/8 fl oz fish or chicken stock
1 tbsp sugar
1 tsp salt
1 tbsp lemon juice
4 tbsp unsalted peanuts, chopped finely,
    plus whole peanuts, to garnish
4 tbsp dried breadcrumbs

NUTRITION
Calories *367*; Sugars *25 g*; Protein *9 g*;
Carbohydrate *33 g*; Fat *23 g*; Saturates *3 g*

easy

8 hrs

7–10 mins

🕊 **COOK'S TIP**

Leave the tails intact on the prawns as this makes them easier to hold when eating.

These little fish cakes are very popular as street food in Thailand and also make a perfect starter with a spicy peanut dip.

Thai Fish Cakes

SERVES 4

350 g/12 oz white fish fillet, such as cod or haddock, skinned
1 tbsp Thai fish sauce
2 tsp Thai red curry paste
1 tbsp lime juice
1 garlic clove, crushed
4 dried kaffir lime leaves, crumbled
1 egg white
3 tbsp chopped fresh coriander
about 125 ml/4 fl oz vegetable oil, for frying
green salad leaves, to serve

peanut dip
1 small fresh red chilli
1 tbsp light soy sauce
1 tbsp lime juice
1 tbsp soft light brown sugar
3 tbsp chunky peanut butter
4 tbsp coconut milk
salt and pepper
snipped fresh chives, to garnish

NUTRITION
Calories 205 g; Sugars 6 g; Protein 17 g; Carbohydrate 7 g; Fat 12 g; Saturates 2 g

easy

15 mins

15 mins

1 Put the fish fillet into a food processor with the Thai fish sauce, red curry paste, lime juice, garlic, lime leaves and egg white and process until a smooth paste forms.

2 Add the chopped coriander and quickly process again until mixed. Divide the mixture into 8–10 pieces and roll into balls between the palms of your hands, then flatten to make small round patties and reserve.

3 To make the dip, halve and deseed the chilli, then chop finely. Place in a small saucepan with the soy sauce, lime juice, sugar, peanut butter and coconut milk and heat gently, stirring constantly, until thoroughly blended. Adjust the seasoning, adding more lime juice or sugar to taste. Transfer to a small bowl, garnish with snipped chives and reserve.

4 Heat the vegetable oil in a frying pan over a medium heat. Add the fish cakes, in batches, and fry for 3–4 minutes on each side until golden-brown. Drain on kitchen paper and serve them hot on a bed of green salad leaves with the chilli-flavoured peanut dip.

These pretty little steamed and fried crab cakes are usually served as a snack, but they also make an appetising starter.

Steamed Crab Cakes

1 Line 8 x 100-ml/3½-fl oz ramekins or foil containers with the banana leaves, cutting them to shape.

2 Mix the garlic, lemon grass, pepper and coriander together in a bowl. Mash the creamed coconut with the lime juice until smooth. Stir it into the other ingredients with the crab meat and Thai fish sauce.

3 Whisk the egg whites in a clean bowl until stiff, then lightly and evenly fold them into the crab mixture. Spoon the mixture into the prepared ramekins or foil containers and press down lightly. Brush the tops with egg yolk and top each with a coriander leaf.

4 Place in a steamer half-filled with boiling water, then cover with a close-fitting lid and steam for 15 minutes or until firm to the touch. Pour off the excess liquid and remove from the ramekins or foil containers.

5 Fill a deep saucepan about one-third full with sunflower oil and heat to 180°C/350°F, or until a cube of bread browns in 30 seconds. Add the crab cakes and deep-fry for about 1 minute, turning them over once, until golden brown. Put the chilli sauce into a small bowl and garnish with chopped coriander. Transfer the crab cakes to a serving plate and serve hot with the chilli sauce.

 COOK'S TIP

For best results, always whisk egg whites in a spotlessly clean, grease-free bowl, otherwise they will not hold their shape very well.

SERVES 4

1–2 banana leaves
2 garlic cloves, crushed
1 tsp chopped finely lemon grass
½ tsp pepper
2 tbsp chopped fresh coriander, plus extra for garnish
3 tbsp creamed coconut
1 tbsp lime juice
200 g/7 oz cooked crab meat, flaked
1 tbsp Thai fish sauce
2 egg whites
1 egg yolk, beaten lightly
8 fresh coriander leaves
600 ml/1 pint sunflower oil, for deep-frying
chilli sauce, to serve

NUTRITION
Calories 156; Sugars 1 g; Protein 13 g;
Carbohydrate 2 g; Fat 11 g; Saturates 4 g

easy

25 mins

20 mins

These crisp, golden-fried little mouthfuls are packed with flavour and served with a hot-and-sweet soy dip – perfect to stimulate appetites at the start of a meal, or as a tasty snack.

Tiger Prawn Rolls

SERVES 4

dip
1 small red bird's-eye chilli, deseeded
1 tsp clear honey
4 tbsp soy sauce

rolls
2 tbsp fresh coriander leaves
1 garlic clove
1½ tsp Thai red curry paste
16 wonton wrappers
1 egg white, beaten lightly
16 raw tiger prawns, peeled with tails intact
600 ml/1 pint sunflower oil, for deep-frying
whole fresh red chillies, to garnish

1 To make the dip, finely chop the chilli, then mix with the honey and soy and stir well. Reserve until required.

2 To make the prawn rolls, finely chop the coriander and garlic, and mix with the red curry paste.

3 Brush each wonton wrapper with egg white and place a small dab of the coriander mixture in the centre. Place a prawn on top.

4 Fold the wonton wrapper over, enclosing the prawn and leaving the tail exposed. Repeat with the other prawns.

5 Fill a deep-fat fryer or deep saucepan about one-third full with sunflower oil and heat to 180°C/350°F, or until a cube of bread turns brown in 30 seconds. Add the prawn rolls in small batches and fry for 1–2 minutes each until golden brown and crisp. Drain on kitchen paper and transfer to a large serving plate. Garnish with fresh chillies and serve with the dip. Give each guest a small bowl filled with hot water and a lemon slice, so that they can wash their fingers afterwards.

NUTRITION
Calories 175; Sugars 2 g; Protein 10 g; Carbohydrate 7 g; Fat 12 g; Saturates 1 g

 easy
 10 mins
10 mins
20 mins

COOK'S TIP
If you prefer, replace the wonton wrappers with filo pastry – use a long strip of pastry, place the paste and a prawn on one end, brush with egg white and wrap the pastry around the prawns to enclose, then fry.

A popular delicacy found throughout many countries in the East, these crisp, golden-fried toasts are very simple to make and perfect to serve with drinks at parties.

Prawn *and* Chicken Sesame Toasts

1 Place the chicken and prawns in a food processor and process until very finely chopped. Add the egg, spring onions, garlic, coriander, Thai fish sauce, pepper and salt, and pulse for a few seconds to mix, then transfer to a bowl.

2 Spread the mixture evenly over the slices of bread, right to the edges. Scatter the sesame seeds over a plate and press the spread side of each slice of bread into them to coat evenly.

3 Using a sharp knife, cut the bread into small rectangles, making 6 per slice.

4 Heat a 1-cm/½-inch depth of sunflower oil in a wide frying pan until very hot. Add the bread rectangles in batches and fry quickly for 2–3 minutes, turning them over once, until golden-brown.

5 Drain the toasts well on kitchen paper and transfer to a large serving dish. Garnish with shredded spring onion curls and serve immediately.

SERVES 4

4 boneless, skinless chicken thighs
100 g/3½ oz cooked peeled prawns
1 small egg, beaten
3 spring onions, chopped finely
2 garlic cloves, crushed
2 tbsp fresh coriander, chopped
1 tbsp Thai fish sauce
½ tsp pepper
¼ tsp salt
12 slices white bread, crusts removed
75 g/2¾ oz/8 tbsp sesame seeds
225 ml/8 fl oz sunflower oil, for shallow-frying
shredded spring onion curls, to garnish

NUTRITION
Calories *491*; Sugars *3 g*; Protein *25 g*; Carbohydrate *39 g*; Fat *27 g*; Saturates *4 g*

easy

10 mins

20 mins

🍳 **COOK'S TIP**

If you're catering for a party, make the toasts in advance. Chill for up to 3 days or place in a sealed container and freeze for up to 1 month. Thaw overnight in the refrigerator, then cook in a hot oven for 5 minutes to reheat thoroughly.

These little pots of shrimps in spicy butter are a classic English dish, originating from Morecambe Bay in Lancashire, where they are still made.

Potted Shrimps

SERVES 4

225 g/8 oz unsalted butter
400 g/14 oz brown shrimps in their shells or 225 g/8 oz cooked peeled prawns
pinch of cayenne pepper
½ tsp ground mace
1 garlic clove, crushed
1 tbsp chopped fresh parsley
salt and pepper
brown bread, to serve

to garnish
lemon wedges
fresh parsley sprigs
cooled whole prawns

NUTRITION
Calories 487; Sugars 0 g; Protein 14 g; Carbohydrate 0.5 g; Fat 48 g; Saturates 31 g

easy

1 hr 30 mins

12 mins

1 Heat the butter in a small saucepan over a low heat until melted and foaming. Reserve for 10 minutes or until the butter separates. Carefully skim off the white milk solids from the clear yellow liquid and discard. The clear yellow oil remaining is clarified butter.

2 Peel the shrimps, discarding the shells. Heat 2 tablespoons of the clarified butter in a frying pan over a low heat. Add the shrimps, then stir in the cayenne, mace and garlic. Increase the heat and stir-fry for 30 seconds until very hot. Remove from the heat, stir in the parsley and season to taste with salt and pepper.

3 Divide the shrimps between 4 small ramekins, pressing down with the back of a spoon. Pour over the remaining clarified butter to cover. Leave to chill in the refrigerator until the butter has set.

4 Remove the ramekins from the refrigerator 30 minutes before serving to allow the butter to soften. Toast the brown bread and transfer to a serving plate. Garnish the shrimps with lemon wedges, fresh parsley sprigs and whole prawns, then serve with the toast.

COOK'S TIP

The most authentic shrimps to use for this recipe are the tiny brown ones. They have a full flavour and soak up the butter well. If your fishmonger can't supply them, substitute the pink peeled variety.

This is a variation on the classic 'Devils on Horseback' – oysters wrapped in bacon. This version uses freshly steamed mussels, stuffed inside marinated prunes, which are then wrapped in smoky bacon and grilled with a sticky glaze.

Prunes Stuffed *with* Mussels

1 Mix the port, honey and garlic together, then season to taste with salt and pepper. Put the prunes into a small bowl and pour over the port mixture. Cover and leave to marinate for at least 4 hours or preferably overnight.

2 Next day, clean the mussels by scrubbing or scraping the shells and pulling out any 'beards' that are attached to them. Put the mussels in a large saucepan with just the water that clings to their shells. Cook, covered, over a high heat for 3–4 minutes until all the mussels have opened. Discard any mussels that remain closed.

3 Strain the mussels, reserving the cooking liquid. Leave to cool, then remove the mussels from their shells.

4 Using the back of a knife, stretch the bacon rashers, then cut in half widthways. Lift the prunes from their marinade, reserving any that remains.

5 Stuff each prune with a mussel, then wrap with a piece of bacon. Secure with a cocktail stick. Repeat to make 24.

6 Simmer the mussel cooking liquid and remaining marinade together in a saucepan until reduced and syrupy. Brush the stuffed prunes with this mixture. Place under a preheated hot grill and cook for 3–4 minutes on each side, turning regularly and brushing with the marinade, until the bacon is crisp and golden. Serve while still hot, with salad leaves.

SERVES 4

3 tbsp port
1 tbsp clear honey
2 garlic cloves, crushed
24 large stoned prunes
24 live mussels
12 rashers smoked streaky bacon
salt and pepper
salad leaves, to serve

NUTRITION
Calories *184*; Sugars *31 g*; Protein *9 g*;
Carbohydrate *33 g*; Fat *1 g*; Saturates *0.5 g*

  easy

  8 hrs 30 mins

10–15 mins

If you find making
mayonnaise difficult, or if
you don't like to eat raw
eggs, use a good-quality
ready-made mayonnaise
and mix in the garlic and
mixed herbs.

Mussel Fritters

S E R V E S   4 – 6

175 g/6 oz plain flour
pinch of salt
1 egg
225 ml/8 fl oz lager
900 g/2 lb live mussels
600 ml/1 pint vegetable oil, for deep-frying

garlic and herb mayonnaise
1 egg yolk
1 tsp Dijon mustard
1 tsp white wine vinegar
2 garlic cloves, crushed
2 tbsp chopped fresh mixed herbs, such as
    parsley, chives, basil and thyme
225 ml/8 fl oz olive oil
salt and pepper

to garnish
lemon slices
fresh parsley sprigs

N U T R I T I O N
Calories 771; Sugars 2 g; Protein 16 g;
Carbohydrate 37 g; Fat 61 g; Saturates 9 g

   easy

   40 mins

   12 mins

1 To make the batter, put the flour into the bowl with the salt. Add the egg
and half the lager and whisk until smooth. Gradually add the remaining
lager, whisking until smooth. Reserve for 30 minutes.

2 Clean the mussels by scrubbing or scraping the shells and pulling out any
'beards' that are attached to them. Discard any with broken shells or any
that refuse to close when tapped. Put the mussels into a large saucepan
with just the water that clings to their shells and cook, covered, over a high
heat for 3–4 minutes, shaking the pan occasionally, until all the mussels
have opened. Discard any mussels that remain closed. Strain and reserve
until cool enough to handle, then remove the mussels from their shells.

3 To make the mayonnaise, put the egg yolk, mustard, vinegar, garlic, herbs
and seasoning into a food processor or blender and process until frothy.
Keeping the machine running, gradually add the olive oil, drop by drop to
begin with, until the mixture begins to thicken. Continue adding the olive oil
in a steady stream until all the oil is incorporated. Season to taste with salt
and pepper and add a little hot water if the mixture seems too thick.
Reserve.

4 Fill a deep saucepan about one-third full with vegetable oil and heat to
190°C/375°F, or until a cube of bread browns in 30 seconds. Drop the mussels,
a few at a time, into the batter and lift out with a slotted spoon. Drop into
the hot oil and cook for 1–2 minutes until crisp and golden. Drain on kitchen
paper. Transfer the fritters to warmed serving plates, garnish with lemon
slices and parsley and serve hot with the mayonnaise.

These delicious morsels make an impressive, yet quick starter. Serve them with some crusty bread to mop up any juices.

Mussels *with* Pesto

1 Clean the mussels by scrubbing or scraping the shells and pulling out any 'beards' that are attached to them. Discard any with broken shells or any that refuse to close when tapped. Put the mussels into a large saucepan with just the water that clings to their shells and cook, covered, over a high heat for 3–4 minutes, shaking the pan occasionally, until all the mussels have opened. Discard any mussels that remain closed. Strain, reserving the cooking liquid, and reserve until cool enough to handle.

2 Strain the cooking liquid into a clean saucepan and simmer over a low heat until reduced to about 1 tablespoon. Put the liquid into a food processor with the basil, garlic, pine kernels and Parmesan cheese and process until finely chopped. Add the olive oil and breadcrumbs and process until mixed.

3 Open the mussels and loosen from their shells, discarding the empty half of the shell. Divide the pesto breadcrumbs between the mussels.

4 Cook under a preheated hot grill until the breadcrumbs are crisp and golden and the mussels heated through. Transfer to a large warmed serving plate. Garnish with tomato slices and basil leaves and serve immediately.

SERVES 4

900 g/2 lb live mussels
6 tbsp chopped fresh basil
2 garlic cloves, crushed
1 tbsp pine kernels, toasted
2 tbsp freshly grated Parmesan cheese
100 ml/3½ fl oz olive oil
115 g/4 oz fresh white breadcrumbs
salt and pepper

to garnish
tomato slices
fresh basil leaves

NUTRITION
Calories 399; Sugars 1 g; Protein 14 g; Carbohydrate 17 g; Fat 31 g; Saturates 5 g

  easy

  20 mins

  12 mins

COOK'S TIP

If you want an alternative to pine kernels add 85 g/3 oz roughly chopped, drained sun-dried tomatoes in oil to the pesto instead.

These small toasts are easy
to prepare and are one
of the most popular
Chinese appetizers in the
West. Make sure you serve
plenty of them as they
are very tasty!

Prawn *and* Sesame Triangles

SERVES 4

225 g/8 oz cooked peeled prawns
1 spring onion
¹⁄₄ tsp salt
1 tsp light soy sauce
1 tbsp cornflour
1 egg white, beaten
3 thin slices white bread, crusts removed
4 tbsp sesame seeds
600 ml/1 pint vegetable oil, for deep-frying

1 Put the prawns and spring onion into a food processor and process until finely chopped. Alternatively, chop them very finely. Transfer to a bowl and stir in the salt, soy sauce, cornflour and egg white.

2 Spread the mixture on to one side of each slice of bread. Spread the sesame seeds on top of the mixture, pressing down well.

3 Cut each slice into 4 equal triangles or strips.

4 Heat the vegetable oil for deep-frying in a preheated wok over a medium–high heat until almost smoking. Carefully place the triangles in the oil, coated side down, and cook for 2–3 minutes until golden-brown. Remove with a slotted spoon and drain on kitchen paper. Serve immediately.

NUTRITION
Calories 237; Sugars 1 g; Protein 18 g;
Carbohydrate 15 g; Fat 12 g; Saturates 2 g

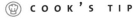

easy
5 mins
10 mins

COOK'S TIP

You could add ¹⁄₂ tsp very finely chopped fresh root ginger and 1 tsp Chinese rice wine to the prawn mixture at the end of step 1, if wished.

The batter may not be traditional, but this is a perfect dish to serve as part of a selection of tapas, or little dishes, with drinks as they do in Spain.

Calamari

1 Sift the flour and salt together into a bowl. Add the eggs and half the soda water and whisk together until smooth. Gradually whisk in the remaining soda water until the batter is smooth. Reserve.

2 To prepare whole squid, hold the body firmly and grasp the tentacles just inside the body. Pull firmly to remove the innards. Find the transparent 'backbone' and remove. Grasp the wings on the outside of the body and pull to remove the outer skin. Trim the tentacles just below the beak and reserve.

3 Wash the body and tentacles under cold running water. Slice the body across into 1-cm/½-inch rings. Drain well on kitchen paper.

4 Meanwhile, fill a deep saucepan about one-third full with vegetable oil and heat to 190°F/375°F, or until a cube of bread browns in 30 seconds.

5 Dip the squid rings and tentacles into the batter, a few at a time, and drop into the hot oil. Fry for 1–2 minutes until crisp and golden. Drain on kitchen paper. Keep warm while you cook the the remaining squid. Transfer the squid to a large serving plate, garnish with lemon wedges and parsley sprigs and serve immediately.

SERVES 4

115 g/4 oz plain flour
1 tsp salt
2 eggs
175 ml/6 fl oz soda water
450 g/1 lb prepared squid (see cook's tip), cut into rings
600 ml/1 pint vegetable oil, for deep-frying

to garnish
lemon wedges
fresh parsley sprigs

NUTRITION
Calories *333*; Sugars *0.5 g*; Protein *24 g*; Carbohydrate *24 g*; Fat *17 g*; Saturates *3 g*

easy
10 mins
10 mins

🥄 COOK'S TIP

If you don't like the idea of cleaning squid yourself, get your fishmonger to do it. Sometimes, squid is even sold already cut into rings. Alternatively, you could use prepared baby squid for this dish.

This is a very typical Greek recipe for stuffing squid. Most large supermarkets with fish counters sell baby squid already cleaned.

Stuffed Squid

SERVES 4

12 baby squid, cleaned
1 tsp salt
4 tbsp olive oil
1 small onion, chopped finely
1 garlic clove, chopped finely
40 g/1½ oz basmati rice
1 tbsp seedless raisins
1 tbsp pine kernels, toasted
1 tbsp chopped fresh flat-leaved parsley
400 g/14 oz canned chopped tomatoes
25 g/1 oz sun-dried tomatoes in oil, drained
   and finely chopped
125 ml/4 fl oz dry white wine
salt and pepper
lemon slices, to garnish
crusty bread, to serve

NUTRITION

Calories *300*; Sugars *9 g*; Protein *12 g*;
Carbohydrate *19 g*; Fat *18 g*; Saturates *2 g*

 moderate

25 mins

1 hr

1 Separate the tentacles from the body of the squid. Chop the tentacles and reserve. Rub the squid tubes inside and out with the salt and reserve while you prepare the stuffing.

2 Heat 1 tablespoon of the olive oil in a frying pan over a low heat. Add the onion and garlic and cook for 4–5 minutes until softened and lightly browned. Add the chopped tentacles and fry for 2–3 minutes. Add the rice, raisins, pine kernels and parsley, then season to taste with salt and pepper. Remove from the heat.

3 Leave the rice mixture to cool slightly, then spoon it into the squid tubes, about three-quarters full to allow the rice to expand. You may need to open the squid tubes a little by making a small cut. Secure each filled squid with a cocktail stick.

4 Heat the remaining oil in a large flameproof casserole over a medium heat. Add the squid and fry for a few minutes on all sides until lightly browned. Add the tomatoes, sun-dried tomatoes, wine and seasoning to taste. Bake in a preheated oven, 180°C/350°F/Gas Mark 4, for 45 minutes. Transfer to a large serving plate, garnish with lemon slices and serve with crusty bread.

COOK'S TIP

If you have difficulty finding baby squid, larger ones work very well and the cooking time is the same. Use cleaned squid weighing 225 g/8 oz in total for the amount of stuffing in this recipe.

Tempura is a classic Japanese batter made with egg, flour and water. The batter mix is very cold and lumpy, which gives the dish its characteristic appearance. It should be eaten straight away.

Tempura Whitebait

1 To make the mayonnaise, put the egg yolk, lime juice, chilli, coriander and seasoning into a food processor or blender and process until foaming. Keeping the machine running, gradually add the olive oil, drop by drop to begin with, until the mixture begins to thicken. Continue adding the olive oil in a steady stream until all the oil is incorporated. Season to taste with salt and pepper and add a little hot water if the mixture seems too thick. Reserve.

2 To make the tempura whitebait, wash the fish under cold running water and pat dry with kitchen paper. Reserve. Sift the flour, cornflour and salt together into a bowl. Whisk the water, egg and ice cubes together and pour on to the flour. Whisk briefly until the mixture is runny, but still lumpy with dry bits of flour still apparent.

3 Meanwhile, fill a deep saucepan about one-third full with vegetable oil and heat to 190°F/375°F, or until a cube of bread browns in 30 seconds.

4 Dip the whitebait, a few at a time, into the batter and carefully drop into the hot oil. Fry for 1 minute until the batter is crisp, but not browned. Drain on kitchen paper. Keep warm while you cook the remaining whitebait. Serve hot with the chilli and lime mayonnaise.

SERVES 4

450 g/1 lb whitebait, thawed if frozen
100 g/3½ oz plain flour
50 g/1¾ oz cornflour
½ tsp salt
200 ml/7 fl oz cold water
1 egg
a few ice cubes
600 ml/1 pint vegetable oil, for deep-frying

chilli and lime mayonnaise

1 egg yolk
1 tbsp lime juice
1 fresh red chilli, deseeded and finely chopped
2 tbsp chopped fresh coriander
200 ml/7 fl oz light olive oil
salt and pepper

NUTRITION
Calories *790*; Sugars *0.5 g*; Protein *23 g*; Carbohydrate *31 g*; Fat *64 g*; Saturates *16 g*

 easy

30 mins

 10 mins

This is a quick and easy
pâté with plenty of flavour.
It originates from Goa, on
the west coast of India,
an area famous for
its seafood.

Smoked Mackerel Pâté

SERVES 4

200 g/7 oz smoked mackerel fillet
1 small, fresh, hot green chilli,
    deseeded and chopped
1 garlic clove, chopped
3 tbsp fresh coriander leaves
150 ml/5 fl oz soured cream
1 small red onion, chopped finely
2 tbsp lime juice
4 slices white bread, crusts removed
salt and pepper

to garnish
fresh dill sprigs
orange slices
lemon slices

1 Skin and flake the mackerel fillet, removing any small bones. Put the flesh into a food processor together with the chilli, garlic, coriander and soured cream and process until smooth.

2 Transfer the mixture to a bowl and mix in the onion and lime juice. Season to taste with salt and pepper. The pâté will seem very soft at this stage but will firm up in the refrigerator. Leave to chill in the refrigerator for several hours or overnight if possible.

3 To make the Melba toasts, place the trimmed bread slices under a preheated medium–hot grill and toast lightly on both sides. Split the toasts in half horizontally, then cut each across diagonally to form 4 triangles per slice.

4 Put the triangles, untoasted side up, under the preheated grill and toast until golden and curled at the edges. To serve, arrange the smoked mackerel pâté on a serving plate and garnish with fresh dill, orange and lemon slices and the Melba toast.

NUTRITION
Calories 316; Sugars 3 g; Protein 13 g;
Carbohydrate 14 g; Fat 23 g; Saturates 8 g

 easy

 4 hrs 30 mins

5 mins

 **COOK'S TIP**

This pâté is also very good served with crudités.

Smoked haddock has an affinity with eggs. Here it is teamed with hard-boiled quail's eggs and topped with a delicious creamy chive dressing.

Smoked Haddock Salad

1 Fill a large frying pan with water and bring to the boil over a medium heat. Add the smoked haddock fillet, cover and remove from the heat. Leave for 10 minutes until the fish is tender. Lift from the poaching water, drain and leave until cool enough to handle. Flake the flesh, removing any small bones. Reserve. Discard the poaching water.

2 Whisk the olive oil, lemon juice, soured cream, hot water, chives and seasoning together. Stir in the tomato. Reserve.

3 Bring a small saucepan of water to the boil over a medium heat. Carefully lower the quail's eggs into the water. Cook the eggs for 3–4 minutes from when the water returns to the boil (3 minutes for a slightly soft centre, 4 minutes for a firm centre). Drain immediately and refresh under cold running water. Carefully peel the eggs, cut in half lengthways and reserve.

4 Toast the bread and cut each across diagonally to form 4 triangles. Arrange 2 halves on each of 4 serving plates. Top with the salad leaves, then the flaked fish and finally the quail's eggs. Spoon over the dressing and garnish with a few sprigs of fresh parsley, lime slices and tomato halves.

SERVES 4

350 g/12 oz smoked haddock fillet
4 tbsp olive oil
1 tbsp lemon juice
2 tbsp soured cream
1 tbsp hot water
2 tbsp snipped fresh chives
1 plum tomato, peeled, deseeded and diced
8 quail's eggs
4 thick slices Granary or multigrain bread
115 g/4 oz mixed salad leaves
salt and pepper

to garnish
fresh flat-leaved parsley sprigs
lime slices
tomatoes, halved

NUTRITION
Calories 223; Sugars 23 g; Protein 21 g; Carbohydrate 25 g; Fat 4 g; Saturates 1 g

easy

15 mins

10 mins

🍴 **COOK'S TIP**

When buying smoked haddock, and smoked fish in general, look for undyed fish, which is always superior in quality.

If you can find them, use small chillies, called bird's-eye, for the dipping sauce. They are extremely hot however, so remove the seeds, if you prefer.

Thai Fish Cakes *with* Dipping Sauce

SERVES 4

450 g/1 lb firm white fish, such as hake or haddock, skinned and chopped roughly
1 tbsp Thai fish sauce
1 tbsp red curry paste (see page 74)
1 kaffir lime leaf, shredded finely
2 tbsp chopped fresh coriander
1 egg
1 tsp brown sugar
large pinch of salt
40 g/1½ oz green beans, sliced thinly crossways
about 125 ml/4 fl oz vegetable oil, for shallow-frying

dipping sauce

4 tbsp sugar
1 tbsp cold water
3 tbsp white rice vinegar
2 small, fresh hot chillies, chopped finely
1 tbsp Thai fish sauce

to garnish

spring onion tassels
fresh chilli flowers

NUTRITION

Calories 223; Sugars 23 g; Protein 21 g; Carbohydrate 25 g; Fat 4 g; Saturates 1 g

easy

15 mins

10 mins

1 To make the fish cakes, put the fish, Thai fish sauce, red curry paste, lime leaf, coriander, egg, sugar and salt into a food processor and process until smooth. Transfer to a small bowl and stir in the green beans. Reserve.

2 To make the dipping sauce, put the sugar, water and rice vinegar into a small saucepan and heat gently over a low heat until the sugar has dissolved. Bring to the boil and simmer for 2 minutes. Remove from the heat and stir in the chillies and Thai fish sauce and leave to cool.

3 Heat a frying pan with enough vegetable oil to generously cover the base of the pan. Divide the fish mixture into 16 little balls. Flatten the balls into patties and fry in the hot oil for 1–2 minutes on each side until golden. Drain on kitchen paper. Transfer to a large serving platter, garnish with spring onion tassels and chilli flowers and serve hot with the dipping sauce.

 COOK'S TIP

It isn't necessary to use the most expensive white fish in this recipe as the other flavours are very strong. Use whatever is cheapest.

These crab cakes contain a high proportion of crab meat and are therefore very light. You can serve them with a warm basil and tomato dressing, but they are also delicious with good-quality mayonnaise.

Maryland Crab Cakes

1 Bring a large saucepan of lightly salted water to the boil over a medium heat. Add the potatoes and cook for 15–20 minutes until tender. Drain well and mash with a fork or potato masher.

2 Mix the crab meat, spring onions, chilli and mayonnaise together in a large bowl. Add the mashed potato and salt and pepper to taste and mix well. Shape the mixture into 8 cakes.

3 Put the flour, egg and breadcrumbs into separate bowls. Dip the cakes first into the flour, then the egg and finally the breadcrumbs to coat. Leave to chill in the refrigerator for 30 minutes.

4 Heat a frying pan with enough vegetable oil to generously cover the base of the pan. Add the cakes, in batches if necessary, and cook for 3–4 minutes on each side until golden and crisp. Drain on kitchen paper and keep warm while you cook the remaining cakes.

5 Meanwhile, to make the dressing, put the olive oil, lemon juice and tomato in a small saucepan and heat gently over a low heat for 2–3 minutes. Remove from the heat and stir in the basil and salt and pepper to taste.

6 Divide the fish cakes between 4 serving plates. Spoon over the dressing and garnish with lemon slices and a few sprigs of fresh dill. Serve immediately.

SERVES 4

225 g/8 oz potatoes, peeled and cut into chunks
450 g/1 lb cooked white and brown crab meat, thawed if frozen
6 spring onions, chopped finely
1 fresh red chilli, deseeded and chopped
3 tbsp mayonnaise
2 tbsp plain flour
1 egg, lightly beaten
115 g/4 oz fresh white breadcrumbs
about 125 ml/4 fl oz vegetable oil, for shallow-frying
salt and pepper

dressing
5 tbsp olive oil
1 tbsp lemon juice
1 large ripe tomato, peeled, deseeded and diced
3 tbsp chopped fresh basil

to garnish
lemon slices
fresh dill sprigs

NUTRITION
Calories *549*; Sugars *3 g*; Protein *29 g*; Carbohydrate *34 g*; Fat *34 g*; Saturates *5 g*

  easy

15 mins

30 mins

You need two pieces of salmon fillet for this dish, approximately the same size. Ask your fishmonger to remove all the bones and scale the fish for you.

Gravadlax

SERVES 4

2 salmon fillets, with skin on, about 450 g/
    1 lb each
6 tbsp chopped fresh dill
115 g/4 oz sea salt
50 g/1¾ oz sugar
1 tbsp white peppercorns, crushed roughly
12 slices brown bread, buttered, to serve

to garnish
lemon slices
fresh dill sprigs

1 Wash the salmon fillets under cold running water and pat dry with kitchen paper. Put one fillet, skin side down, in a non-metallic dish.

2 Mix the dill, sea salt, sugar and peppercorns together. Spread this mixture over the first fillet of fish and place the second fillet, skin side up, on top. Put a plate, the same size as the fish, on top and put a weight on the plate.

3 Leave to chill in the refrigerator for 2 days, turning the fish about every 12 hours and basting with any juices, that have come out of the fish.

4 Remove the salmon from the brine and slice thinly, without slicing the skin, as you would smoked salmon. Cut the brown bread into triangles. Arrange the salmon slices and brown bread on 4 serving plates and garnish with lemon slices and a few sprigs of fresh dill. Serve.

NUTRITION
Calories *608*; Sugars *11 g*; Protein *37 g*;
Carbohydrate *41 g*; Fat *34 g*; Saturates *14 g*

 easy

 48 hrs 30 mins

0 mins

COOK'S TIP

You can brush the marinade off the salmon before slicing, but the line of green along the edge of the salmon is quite attractive and, of course, full of flavour.

Don't be put off by the long list of ingredients. The omelette is served cold and so can be made entirely ahead of time.

Thai Crab Omelette

1 Put the crab meat into a bowl and check for any small pieces of shell. Add the spring onions, coriander, chives and cayenne and reserve.

2 Heat the vegetable oil in a large frying pan over a low heat. Add the garlic, ginger and chilli and stir-fry for 30 seconds. Add the lime juice, lime leaves, sugar and Thai fish sauce. Simmer for 3–4 minutes until reduced. Remove from the heat and leave to cool. Add to the crab mixture and reserve.

3 Lightly beat the eggs with the coconut cream and salt. Heat the vegetable oil in a large frying pan over a medium heat. Add the egg mixture and as it sets on the base, carefully pull the edges in toward the centre, allowing the unset egg to run underneath.

4 When the egg is nearly set, spoon the crab mixture down the centre. Cook for a further 1–2 minutes to finish cooking the egg, then turn the omelette out of the pan on to a serving dish. Leave to cool, then leave to chill in the refrigerator for 2–3 hours or overnight. Cut into 4 pieces and garnish with shredded spring onion to serve.

SERVES 4

225 g/8 oz white crab meat, fresh or thawed if frozen
3 spring onions, chopped finely
1 tbsp chopped fresh coriander
1 tbsp snipped fresh chives
pinch of cayenne pepper
1 tbsp vegetable oil
2 garlic cloves, crushed
1 tsp freshly grated root ginger
1 red chilli, deseeded and finely chopped
2 tbsp lime juice
2 lime leaves, shredded
2 tsp sugar
2 tsp Thai fish sauce
3 eggs
4 tbsp coconut cream
1 tsp salt
1 tbsp vegetable oil
shredded spring onion, to garnish

NUTRITION
Calories *262*; Sugars *5 g*; Protein *18 g*;
Carbohydrate *5 g*; Fat *19 g*; Saturates *7 g*

 moderate

 2 hrs 30 mins

35 mins

 COOK'S TIP

You can serve this omelette warm. After adding the crab, cook for 3–4 minutes to let the mixture heat through, then serve immediately.

Soups *and* Stews

Using seafood in soups and stews makes wonderful sense. It doesn't require much cooking, making it ideal as a basis for a mid-week supper, and it combines well with an enormous variety of flavours.

It seems that only in English-speaking countries is fish undervalued. Other parts of the world use fish as a staple part of their diet and this chapter includes many dishes from a variety of places. Don't worry, though – most of the more unusual ingredients are readily available nowadays from larger supermarkets or from specialist shops.

Soups like Thai Fish Soup and Chinese Crab & Sweetcorn Soup illustrate the diversity of the recipes. Some of the soups, such as the Creamy Scallop Soup, are very subtly flavoured and would be ideal as a first course at a dinner party.

This is also known as Tom Yam Gung. Oriental supermarkets may sell tom yam sauce ready prepared in jars, sometimes labelled 'Chillies in Oil'.

Thai Fish Soup

SERVES 4

450 ml/16 fl oz light chicken stock
2 kaffir lime leaves, chopped
5-cm/2-inch piece of lemon grass, chopped
3 tbsp lemon juice
3 tbsp Thai fish sauce
2 small, fresh hot green chillies, deseeded and finely chopped
½ tsp sugar
8 small shiitake mushrooms, halved
450 g/1 lb raw prawns, peeled if necessary and deveined
shredded spring onions, to garnish

tom yam sauce

4 tbsp vegetable oil
5 garlic cloves, chopped finely
1 large shallot, chopped finely
2 large, hot dried red chillies, chopped
1 tbsp dried shrimp, optional
1 tbsp Thai fish sauce
2 tsp sugar

NUTRITION

Calories 230; Sugars 4 g; Protein 22 g;
Carbohydrate 9 g; Fat 12 g; Saturates 1 g

  moderate

25 mins

5 mins

1 To make the tom yam sauce, heat the vegetable oil in a small saucepan over a low heat. Add the garlic and cook briefly until just browned, remove with a slotted spoon and reserve. Add the shallot and cook until browned and crisp. Remove with a slotted spoon and reserve. Add the chillies and fry until they darken. Remove and drain on kitchen paper. Remove the pan from the heat, reserving the oil for later use.

2 Put the dried shrimp (if using) into a small food processor or spice grinder and grind, then add the reserved chillies, garlic and shallot. Grind to a smooth paste. Return the paste to the original pan over a low heat. Mix in the Thai fish sauce and sugar. Remove from the heat.

3 Heat the stock and 2 tablespoons of the tom yam sauce in a large saucepan over a low heat. Add the lime leaves, lemon grass, lemon juice, Thai fish sauce, chillies and sugar. Simmer for 2 minutes.

4 Add the mushrooms and prawns and cook for a further 2–3 minutes until the prawns are cooked. Ladle into 4 warmed bowls, garnish with shredded spring onion and serve immediately.

COOK'S TIP

Some of the 'kick' can be taken out of the chillies by removing the seeds and membrane. Cut fresh chillies in half and scrape out the seeds. Cut the end off dried chillies and shake out the seeds. Wash your hands after handling chillies.

This delicious soup has a real 'kick' of red hot chillies, perfect to warm up a winter's day. If you prefer a milder flavour, remove the seeds from the chillies before using them.

Chilli-spiced Prawn Wonton Soup

1 Finely chop the prawns. Put them into a bowl and stir in the garlic, spring onion, soy sauce, Thai fish sauce, coriander and egg yolk.

2 Lay the wonton wrappers on a work surface in a single layer and place about 1 tablespoon of the filling mixture in the centre of each. Brush the edges with egg white and fold each one into a triangle, pressing lightly to seal. Bring the 2 bottom corners of the triangle around to meet in the centre, securing with a little egg white to hold in place.

3 To make the soup, slice the chillies at a steep diagonal angle to make long thin slices, removing the seeds, if you prefer. Slice the spring onions on the same angle.

4 Place the stock, Thai fish sauce, soy sauce and Chinese rice wine in a large saucepan and bring to the boil over a medium heat. Add the chillies and spring onions. Drop the wontons into the pan and simmer for 4–5 minutes until thoroughly heated.

5 Ladle the soup and wontons into 4 small bowls, garnish with fresh coriander leaves scattered over at the last moment and serve immediately.

SERVES 4

wontons
175 g/6 oz cooked prawns, peeled
1 garlic clove, crushed
1 spring onion, chopped finely
1 tbsp dark soy sauce
1 tbsp Thai fish sauce
1 tbsp fresh coriander, chopped
1 small egg, separated
12 wonton wrappers

soup
2 small red bird's-eye chillies
2 spring onions
1 litre/1¾ pints clear beef stock
1 tbsp Thai fish sauce
1 tbsp dark soy sauce
1 tbsp Chinese rice wine
handful of fresh coriander leaves, to garnish

NUTRITION
Calories *83*; Sugars *0.5 g*; Protein *13 g*;
Carbohydrate *4 g*; Fat *2 g*; Saturates *0.5 g*

⭐⭐   easy

     10 mins

     8 mins

Hot and sour mixtures are popular throughout the East, especially in Thailand. This soup typically has either prawns or chicken added, but tofu can be used instead if you prefer a meatless version.

Hot *and* Sour Soup

SERVES 4

350 g/12 oz whole raw or cooked prawns in shells
1 tbsp vegetable oil
1 lemon grass stalk, chopped roughly
2 kaffir lime leaves, shredded
1 fresh green chilli, deseeded and chopped
1.2 litres/2 pints chicken or fish stock
1 lime
1 tbsp Thai fish sauce
1 red bird's-eye chilli, deseeded and thinly sliced
1 spring onion, sliced thinly
salt and pepper
1 tbsp fresh coriander, chopped finely, to garnish

1 Peel the prawns and reserve the shells. Devein the prawns, cover and leave to chill in the refrigerator.

2 Heat the vegetable oil in a large frying pan over a medium heat. Add the prawn shells and stir-fry for 3–4 minutes until they turn pink. Add the lemon grass, lime leaves, chilli and stock. Pare a thin strip of rind from the lime and grate the rest. Add the grated rind to the pan.

3 Bring to the boil, then reduce the heat, cover and simmer for 20 minutes.

4 Strain the liquid through a sieve and pour it back into the pan. Squeeze the juice from the lime and add to the pan with the Thai fish sauce and salt and pepper to taste.

5 Return to the boil, then reduce the heat, add the prawns and simmer for about 2–3 minutes.

6 Add the thinly sliced chilli and spring onion. Ladle into 4 warmed serving bowls, sprinkle with chopped coriander and serve.

NUTRITION
Calories 71; Sugars *0 g*; Protein *8 g*;
Carbohydrate *1 g*; Fat *4 g*; Saturates *0 g*

easy

15 mins

30 mins

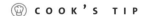 **COOK'S TIP**

To devein the prawns, remove the shells. Cut a slit along the back of each prawn and remove the fine black vein that runs along the length of the back. Wipe with kitchen paper.

This is a traditional, creamy Scottish soup. As the smoked haddock has quite a strong flavour, it has been mixed with some fresh cod.

Cullen Skink

1 Put the haddock fillet into a large frying pan and cover with boiling water. Leave for 10 minutes. Drain, reserving 300 ml/10 fl oz of the soaking water. Flake the fish, taking care to remove all the bones.

2 Heat the butter in a large saucepan over a low heat. Add the onion and cook gently for 10 minutes until softened. Add the milk and bring to a gentle simmer before adding the potatoes. Cook for 10 minutes.

3 Add the reserved haddock flakes and cod. Simmer for a further 10 minutes until the cod is tender.

4 Remove about one-third of the fish and potatoes, put into a food processor and process until smooth. Alternatively, rub through a sieve into a bowl. Return to the soup with the cream, parsley and salt and pepper to taste. Taste and add a little lemon juice, if wished. Add a little of the reserved soaking water if the soup seems too thick. Reheat gently, then ladle into 4 warmed soup bowls, garnish with lemon slices and a few sprigs of fresh parsley, then serve immediately.

SERVES 4

225 g/8 oz undyed smoked haddock fillet
2 tbsp butter
1 onion, chopped finely
600 ml/1 pint milk
350 g/12 oz potatoes, peeled and diced
350 g/12 oz cod, boned, skinned and cubed
150 ml/5 fl oz double cream
2 tbsp chopped fresh parsley
lemon juice, to taste
salt and pepper

to garnish
lemon slices
fresh parsley sprigs

NUTRITION
Calories *108*; Sugars *2.3 g*; Protein *7.4 g*;
Carbohydrate *5.6 g*; Fat *6.4 g*; Saturates *4 g*

 moderate

20 mins

 40 mins

 COOK'S TIP

Look for Finnan haddock, if you can find it. Traditionally cured over peat smoke, it can be eaten by itself or included in omelettes or dishes such as kedgeree.

A chowder is a thick soup whose main ingredients are milk and potatoes, to which other flavours are added. This is a classic version from New England, flavoured with fresh clams.

New England Clam Chowder

SERVES 4

900 g/2 lb live clams
4 rashers rindless streaky bacon, chopped
25 g/1 oz butter
1 onion, chopped
1 tbsp chopped fresh thyme
1 large potato, peeled and diced
300 ml/10 fl oz milk
1 bay leaf
150 ml/5 fl oz double cream
1 tbsp chopped fresh parsley
salt and pepper

NUTRITION
Calories *136*; Sugars *2 g*; Protein *7.7 g*;
Carbohydrate *5.4 g*; Fat *9.5 g*; Saturates *5.4 g*

⭐⭐   easy

🕐   15 mins

🕐   30 mins

1 Scrub the clams and put into a large saucepan with a splash of water. Cook over a high heat for 3–4 minutes until all the clams have opened. Discard any that remain closed. Strain the clams, reserving the cooking liquid. Leave until cool enough to handle.

2 Reserve 8 clams in their shells for garnish, then remove the rest of the clams from their shells. Roughly chop if large, and reserve.

3 Dry-fry the bacon in a clean saucepan over a medium–low heat until browned and crisp. Drain on kitchen paper. Add the butter to the same pan and when it has melted, add the onion. Cook for 4–5 minutes until softened, but not coloured. Add the thyme and cook briefly before adding the diced potato, reserved clam cooking liquid, milk and bay leaf. Bring to the boil and simmer for 10 minutes until the potato is tender, but not falling apart. Transfer to a food processor and process until smooth. Alternatively, rub through a sieve into a bowl and return to the pan.

4 Add the clams, bacon and cream. Simmer for 2–3 minutes until heated through. Season to taste with salt and pepper. Stir in the parsley and ladle into 4 soup bowls. Garnish with the reserved clams in their shells and serve.

 **COOK'S TIP**

You can, if you wish, add 2 large skinned tomatoes with the thyme in Step 3 and omit the cream in Step 4.

Packed full of flavour, this delicious fish soup makes a meal in itself when it is accompanied by a crisp mixed green salad.

Fish *and* Crab Chowder

1 Place the onion, celery and wine in a large non-stick saucepan. Bring to the boil, cover and cook over a low heat for 5 minutes.

2 Uncover the pan and cook for a further 5 minutes until almost all the liquid has evaporated.

3 Pour in the stock and milk and add the bay leaf. Bring to a simmer and stir in the cod and haddock. Simmer over a low heat, uncovered, for 5 minutes.

4 Add the crab meat, French beans and cooked brown rice and simmer gently for 2–3 minutes until just heated through. Remove the bay leaf with a slotted spoon and discard.

5 Stir in the cornflour mixture and heat, stirring, until thickened slightly. Season to taste with salt and pepper and ladle into 4 large, warmed soup bowls. Serve with a mixed green salad.

SERVES 4

1 large onion, chopped finely
2 celery sticks, chopped finely
150 ml/5 fl oz dry white wine
600 ml/1 pint fish stock
600 ml/1 pint skimmed milk
1 bay leaf
225 g/8 oz smoked cod fillet, skinned and cut into 2.5-cm/1-inch cubes
225 g/8 oz smoked haddock fillets, skinned and cut into 2.5-cm/1-inch cubes
350 g/12 oz canned crab meat, drained
225 g/8 oz blanched French beans, sliced into 2.5-cm/1-inch pieces
225 g/8 oz cooked brown rice
4 tsp cornflour mixed with 4 tbsp water
salt and pepper
mixed green salad, to serve

NUTRITION
Calories *440*; Sugars *10 g*; Protein *49 g*; Carbohydrate *43 g*; Fat *7 g*; Saturates *1 g*

 easy

 40 mins

40 mins

25 mins

This soup is based on the classic Chinese chicken and sweetcorn soup, but the delicate flavour of the crab works very well.

Chinese Crab *and* Sweetcorn Soup

SERVES 4

1 tbsp vegetable oil
1 small onion, chopped finely
1 garlic clove, chopped finely
1 tsp grated fresh root ginger
1 small, fresh red chilli, deseeded
   and finely chopped
2 tbsp dry sherry or Chinese rice wine
225 g/8 oz fresh white crab meat
320 g/11 oz canned sweetcorn, drained
600 ml/1 pint light chicken stock
1 tbsp light soy sauce
2 tbsp chopped fresh coriander
2 eggs, beaten
salt and pepper
fresh red chilli tassels, to garnish

1 Heat the vegetable oil in a large saucepan over a low heat. Add the onion and cook gently for 5 minutes until softened. Add the garlic, ginger and chilli and cook for a further 1 minute.

2 Add the sherry or Chinese rice wine and bubble until reduced by half. Add the crab meat, sweetcorn, chicken stock and soy sauce. Bring to the boil and simmer gently for 5 minutes. Stir in the coriander. Season to taste with salt and pepper.

3 Remove from the heat and pour in the eggs. Wait for a few seconds and then stir well, to break the eggs into ribbons. Ladle into 4 large, warmed soup bowls, garnish with fresh chilli tassels and serve immediately.

NUTRITION
Calories *440 g*; Sugars *10 g*; Protein *49 g*;
Carbohydrate *43 g*; Fat *7 g*; Saturates *1 g*

 easy

40 mins

25 mins

 COOK'S TIP

For convenience, you could use canned crab meat. Make sure it is well drained before adding it to the soup.

This is a very delicately flavoured soup which, like all seafood, should not be overcooked. A sprinkling of parsley just before serving makes a pretty contrast to the creamy colour of the soup.

Creamy Scallop Soup

1 Melt the butter in a large saucepan over a very low heat. Add the onion and cook for 10 minutes until softened, but not coloured. Add the potatoes and salt and pepper to taste, cover and cook for a further 10 minutes.

2 Pour on the stock, bring to the boil and simmer for a further 10–15 minutes until the potatoes are tender.

3 Meanwhile, prepare the scallops. If the corals are available, roughly chop and reserve. Roughly chop the white meat and put into a second saucepan with the milk. Bring to a gentle simmer and cook for 6–8 minutes until the scallops are just tender.

4 When the potatoes are cooked, transfer them and their cooking liquid to a food processor or blender and process to a purée. Alternatively, rub through a sieve. Return the mixture to a clean saucepan with the scallops and their milk and the pieces of coral (if using).

5 Remove the pan from the heat. Whisk the egg yolks and cream together and add to the soup. Return to a very gentle heat and, stirring constantly, reheat the soup until thickened slightly. Do not boil or it will curdle. Adjust the seasoning to taste. Ladle into 4 soup bowls, sprinkle with parsley and serve.

COOK'S TIP

The soup can be made in advance up to the point where the cream and eggs are added. This should only be done just before serving.

SERVES 4

50 g/1¾ oz butter
1 onion, chopped finely
450 g/1 lb potatoes, peeled and diced
600 ml/1 pint hot fish stock
350 g/12 oz prepared scallops, including corals if available
300 ml/10 fl oz milk
2 egg yolks
90 ml/3¼ fl oz double cream
salt and pepper
1 tbsp chopped fresh parsley, to garnish

NUTRITION
Calories 9.8; Sugars 1.4 g; Protein 6.5 g; Carbohydrate 5.9 g; Fat 5.6 g; Saturates 3.2 g

 easy

 10 mins

35 mins

Surprisingly, this soup is French in origin. This version, however, uses freshly roasted spices rather than the bland curry powder that is so popular.

Curried Mussel Soup

S E R V E S 4

½ tsp coriander seeds
½ tsp cumin seeds
900 g/2 lb live mussels
100 ml/3½ fl oz white wine
50 g/1¾ oz butter
1 onion, chopped finely
1 garlic clove, chopped finely
1 tsp freshly grated root ginger
1 tsp turmeric
pinch of cayenne pepper
600 ml/1 pint fish stock
4 tbsp double cream
25 g/1 oz butter, softened
25 g/1 oz plain flour
salt and pepper
2 tbsp chopped fresh parsley, to garnish

N U T R I T I O N
Calories *391*; Sugars *3 g*; Protein *11 g*;
Carbohydrate *11 g*; Fat *32 g*; Saturates *20 g*

  easy

  5 mins

 30 mins

1 Dry-fry the coriander and cumin seeds in a frying pan over a medium heat until they begin to smell aromatic and start to pop. Transfer to a mortar and grind to a powder with a pestle. Reserve.

2 Clean the mussels by scrubbing or scraping the shells and pulling out any beards that are attached to them. Discard any with broken shells or any that refuse to close when tapped. Put the mussels into a large saucepan with the wine and cook, covered, over a high heat for 3–4 minutes, shaking the pan occasionally, until all the mussels have opened. Discard any mussels that remain closed. Strain, reserving the cooking liquid, and leave until the mussels are cool enough to handle. Remove about two-thirds of the mussels from their shells and reserve all the mussels. Strain the mussel cooking liquid through a fine sieve.

3 Heat half the butter in a large saucepan over a low heat. Add the onion and fry gently for 4–5 minutes until softened, but not coloured. Add the garlic and ginger and cook for a further 1 minute before adding the roasted and ground spices, the turmeric and cayenne. Fry for 1 minute before adding the fish stock, reserved mussel cooking liquid and cream. Simmer for 10 minutes.

4 Cream the butter and flour together to form a thick paste. Add the paste to the simmering soup and stir until dissolved and until the soup has thickened slightly. Add the mussels and warm for 2 minutes. Ladle into 4 warmed soup bowls, garnish with parsley and serve.

This recipe is intended to be served in small quantities. It is very rich and full of flavour.

Clam *and* Sorrel Soup

1 Put the clams into a large saucepan with the onion and wine. Cover and cook over a high heat for 3–4 minutes until the clams have opened. Strain, reserving the cooking liquid, but discarding the onion. Leave the clams until they are cool enough to handle. Remove from their shells.

2 Melt the butter in a clean saucepan over a low heat. Add the carrot, shallots and celery and cook very gently for 10 minutes until softened, but not coloured. Add the reserved cooking liquid and bay leaves and simmer for a further 10 minutes.

3 Meanwhile, roughly chop the clams, if large. Add to the soup with the cream and sorrel. Simmer for a further 2–3 minutes until the sorrel has collapsed. Season with pepper and ladle into 4 warmed soup bowls. Garnish with a few sprigs of fresh dill and serve immediately.

SERVES 4

900 g/2 lb live clams, scrubbed
1 onion, chopped finely
150 ml/5 fl oz dry white wine
50 g/1¾ oz butter
1 small carrot, diced finely
2 shallots, diced finely
1 celery stick, diced finely
2 bay leaves
150 ml/5 fl oz double cream
25 g/1 oz loosely packed shredded sorrel
pepper
fresh dill sprigs, to garnish

NUTRITION
Calories *384*; Sugars *4 g*; Protein *18 g*;
Carbohydrate *7 g*; Fat *29 g*; Saturates *18 g*

moderate

10–15 mins

30 mins

🍲 **COOK'S TIP**

Sorrel is a large-leaved herb with a slightly sour, lemony flavour that goes very well with fish. It is increasingly easy to find in larger supermarkets, but is also incredibly easy to grow as a plant.

Use any fish that is available for this soup. Good fish to choose might include eel, skate or cod. Avoid oily fish such as mackerel, herring and also salmon.

Fish *and* Bread Soup

SERVES 6 – 8

1.7 kg/4 lb mixed whole fish
225 g/8 oz raw prawns
2.2 litres/4 pints water
150 ml/5 fl oz olive oil
2 large onions, chopped roughly
2 celery sticks, chopped roughly
1 leek, chopped roughly
1 small fennel bulb, chopped roughly
5 garlic cloves, chopped
3 tbsp orange juice, plus 1 strip orange peel
400 g/14 oz canned chopped tomatoes
1 red pepper, deseeded and sliced
1 fresh thyme sprig
large pinch of saffron threads
6–8 thick slices sourdough bread
salt and pepper

red pepper and saffron sauce
1 red pepper, deseeded and quartered
150 ml/5 fl oz olive oil
1 egg yolk
large pinch of saffron threads
pinch of crushed chillies

NUTRITION
Calories 755; Sugars 9 g; Protein 46 g;
Carbohydrate 23 g; Fat 54 g; Saturates 9 g

⭐⭐   easy

     40 mins

🕐   1 hr 10 mins

1 Fillet the fish, reserving all the bones. Roughly chop the flesh. Peel the prawns. Place the fish bones and the shells in a large saucepan with the water and bring to the boil. Simmer for 20 minutes, then strain.

2 Heat the olive oil in a large pan over a low heat. Add the onions, celery, leek, fennel and garlic and cook gently for 20 minutes without colouring. Add the orange juice and peel, tomatoes, red pepper, thyme, saffron, prawns and fish fillets and strained stock, bring to the boil and simmer for 40 minutes.

3 To prepare the sauce. Brush the red pepper quarters with some of the olive oil. Place under a preheated hot grill for 8–10 minutes, turning once, until the skins have blackened and the flesh is tender. Put in a polythene bag.

4 Once cool, peel off the skin. Roughly chop the flesh and place in a food processor with the egg yolk, saffron, crushed chillies and seasoning. Process until the pepper is smooth. Gradually add the olive oil, in a slow stream, until the sauce begins to thicken. Continue adding the oil in a steady stream until all the oil is incorporated. Season to taste with salt and pepper, if necessary.

5 When the soup is cooked, put into a food processor or blender and process until smooth, then rub through a sieve. Return to the heat and season to taste with salt and pepper.

6 Toast the bread on both sides and place in the base of the soup plates. Ladle over the soup and serve with the sauce.

Although versions of this stew are eaten throughout Spain, it originated in the Basque region and would have been largely prepared and eaten by fishermen.

Basque Tuna Stew

1 Heat 2 tablespoons of the olive oil in a saucepan over a low heat. Add the onion and cook for 8–10 minutes until softened and browned. Add the garlic and cook a further 1 minute. Add the tomatoes, cover and simmer for about 30 minutes until thickened.

2 Meanwhile, mix the potatoes and peppers together in a large, clean saucepan. Add the water, which should just cover the vegetables. Bring to the boil over a medium heat and simmer for 15 minutes until the potatoes are almost tender.

3 Add the tuna chunks and the tomato mixture to the potatoes and peppers and season to taste with salt and pepper. Cover and simmer for 6–8 minutes until the tuna is tender.

4 Meanwhile, heat the remaining olive oil in a large frying pan over a medium heat. Add the bread slices and fry on both sides until golden. Drain on kitchen paper. Transfer the stew to 4 large, warmed serving bowls and serve with the toast, if wished.

SERVES 4

5 tbsp olive oil
1 large onion, chopped
2 garlic cloves, chopped
200 g/7 oz canned chopped tomatoes
700 g/1 lb 9 oz potatoes, peeled and cut into
   5-cm/2-inch chunks
3 green peppers, deseeded
   and roughly chopped
300 ml/10 fl oz cold water
900 g/2 lb fresh tuna, cut into chunks
4 slices crusty white bread, optional
salt and pepper

NUTRITION
Calories 718; Sugars 9 g; Protein 63 g;
Carbohydrate 2 g; Fat 6 g; Saturates 1 g

easy

5 mins

20 mins

🎩 COOK'S TIP

Substitute any very firm-fleshed fish, such as shark or swordfish, for the tuna used in this recipe.

Goan cuisine is famous for seafood and for vindaloo dishes, which tend to be very hot. This is a milder dish, but also very flavourful.

Goan Fish Curry

SERVES 4

750 g/1 lb 10 oz monkfish fillet, cut into chunks
1 tbsp cider vinegar
½ tsp salt
1 tsp ground turmeric
3 tbsp vegetable oil
2 garlic cloves, crushed
1 small onion, chopped finely
2 tsp ground coriander
1 tsp cayenne pepper
2 tsp paprika
2 tbsp tamarind pulp, plus 2 tbsp boiling water (see method)
85 g/3 oz creamed coconut, cut into pieces
300 ml/10 fl oz warm water
fresh coriander leaves, to garnish
plain boiled rice, to serve

NUTRITION

Calories *302*; Sugars *7 g*; Protein *31 g*;
Carbohydrate *8 g*; Fat *17 g*; Saturates *7 g*

 easy

 30 mins

12 mins

1 Put the fish on a plate and drizzle over the vinegar. Mix the salt and half the turmeric together and sprinkle evenly over the fish. Cover and leave to stand for 20 minutes.

2 Heat the vegetable oil in a frying pan over a low heat. Add the garlic and cook until browned slightly, then add the onion and fry for 3–4 minutes until softened, but not browned. Add the ground coriander and stir for 1 minute.

3 Mix the remaining turmeric, cayenne and paprika with about 2 tablespoons of water to make a paste. Add to the pan and cook over a low heat for about 1–2 minutes.

4 Mix the tamarind pulp with the boiling water and stir well. When the water appears thick and the pulp has come away from the seeds, rub this mixture through a sieve, rubbing the pulp well. Discard the seeds once finished.

5 Add the coconut, warm water and tamarind paste to the pan and stir until the coconut has dissolved. Add the pieces of fish and any juices on the plate and simmer gently for 4–5 minutes until the sauce has thickened and the fish is just tender. Garnish with coriander and serve immediately on a bed of plain boiled rice.

The pale green curry paste in this recipe can be used as the basis for all sorts of Thai fish dishes. It is also delicious with chicken and beef.

Thai Green Fish Curry

1 To make the curry paste, put all the ingredients into a blender or spice grinder and blend to a smooth paste, adding a little water, if necessary. Alternatively, pound the ingredients, using a mortar and pestle, until smooth. Reserve.

2 Heat the vegetable oil in a large frying pan or preheated wok over a medium heat until almost smoking. Add the garlic and fry until golden. Add the curry paste and stir-fry a few seconds before adding the aubergine. Stir-fry for about 4–5 minutes until softened.

3 Add the coconut cream, bring to the boil and stir until the cream thickens and curdles slightly. Add the Thai fish sauce and sugar to the frying pan and stir well.

4 Add the fish pieces and stock. Simmer for 3–4 minutes, stirring occasionally, until the fish is just tender. Add the lime leaves and basil, then cook for a further 1 minute. Transfer to a large, warmed serving dish and garnish with a few sprigs of fresh dill. Serve immediately.

SERVES 4

2 tbsp vegetable oil
1 garlic clove, chopped
1 small aubergine, diced
120 ml/4 fl oz coconut cream
2 tbsp Thai fish sauce
1 tsp sugar
225 g/8 oz firm white fish, cut into pieces
125 ml/4 fl oz fish stock
2 kaffir lime leaves, shredded finely
about 15 leaves fresh Thai basil
fresh dill sprigs, to garnish

green curry paste

5 fresh green chillies, deseeded and chopped
2 tsp chopped lemon grass
1 large shallot, chopped
2 garlic cloves, chopped
1 tsp freshly grated root ginger or galangal
2 fresh coriander roots, chopped
½ tsp ground coriander
¼ tsp ground cumin
1 kaffir lime leaf, chopped finely
½ tsp salt

NUTRITION
Calories 217; Sugars 3 g; Protein 12 g;
Carbohydrate 5 g; Fat 17 g; Saturates 10 g

 easy

 5 mins

5 mins

15 mins

This is a very simple dish which uses a variety of spices and readily available ingredients.

Haddock Baked *in* Yogurt

SERVES 4

2 large onions, sliced thinly
900 g/2 lb haddock fillet, from the head end
425 ml/15 fl oz natural yogurt
2 tbsp lemon juice
1 tsp sugar
2 tsp ground cumin
2 tsp ground coriander
pinch of garam masala
pinch of cayenne pepper, to taste
1 tsp freshly grated root ginger
3 tbsp vegetable oil
50 g/1¾ oz cold unsalted butter,
    cut into pieces
salt and pepper
fresh parsley sprigs, to garnish

to serve
boiled new potatoes
freshly cooked mangetouts

NUTRITION
Calories *448*; Sugars *16 g*; Protein *47 g*;
Carbohydrate *20 g*; Fat *21 g*; Saturates *8 g*

easy

20 mins

40 mins

1 Line a large baking dish with the onion slices. Cut the fish into strips widthways and lay the fish in a single layer over the onions.

2 Mix the yogurt, lemon juice, sugar, cumin, coriander, garam masala, cayenne, ginger, vegetable oil and seasoning together in a small bowl. Pour the sauce over the fish, making sure it goes under the fish as well. Cover tightly.

3 Bake in a preheated oven, 190°C/375°F/Gas Mark 5, for 30 minutes or until the fish is just tender.

4 Carefully pour the sauce off the fish and into a saucepan. Bring to the boil over a low heat and simmer to reduce the sauce to about 350 ml/12 fl oz. Remove the pan from the heat.

5 Add the cubes of butter to the sauce and whisk until melted and incorporated. Pour the sauce back over the fish and transfer to 4 large, warmed serving plates. Garnish with a few sprigs of fresh parsley and serve with boiled new potatoes and mangetouts.

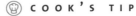 **COOK'S TIP**

When you pour the sauce off the fish it will look thin and separated, but reducing and stirring in the butter will help to amalgamate it.

Not strictly authentic, but this dish uses the typical Italian flavours of tomatoes, capers, olives and basil to make a delicious supper dish.

Cod Italienne

1 Heat the olive oil in a large saucepan over a low heat. Add the onion and fry gently for 5 minutes until softened, but not coloured. Add the garlic and thyme and cook for a further 1 minute.

2 Add the red wine and increase the heat. Simmer until reduced and syrupy. Add the tomatoes and sugar and bring to the boil. Cover and simmer for about 30 minutes. Uncover and simmer for a further 20 minutes until thick. Stir in the olives, capers and basil. Season to taste with salt and pepper.

3 Arrange the cod steaks in a shallow ovenproof dish and spoon the tomato sauce over the top. Bake in a preheated oven, 190°C/375°F/Gas Mark 5 for 20–25 minutes until the fish is just tender.

4 Remove from the oven and arrange the mozzarella slices on top of the fish.

5 Return to the oven for a further 5–10 minutes until the cheese has melted. Transfer to 4 large, warmed serving plates and garnish with a few sprigs of fresh coriander and lime slices. Serve immediately.

SERVES 4

2 tbsp olive oil
1 onion, chopped finely
2 garlic cloves, chopped finely
2 tsp freshly chopped thyme
150 ml/5 fl oz red wine
800 g /1 lb 12 oz canned chopped tomatoes
pinch of sugar
50 g/1¾ oz stoned black olives, chopped roughly
50 g/1¾ oz stoned green olives, chopped roughly
2 tbsp capers, drained, rinsed and roughly chopped
2 tbsp chopped fresh basil
4 cod steaks, about 175 g/6 oz each
150 g/5½ oz mozzarella cheese, sliced
salt and pepper

to garnish
fresh coriander sprigs
lime slices

NUTRITION
Calories *387*; Sugars *8 g*; Protein *44 g*; Carbohydrate *10 g*; Fat *16 g*; Saturates *6 g*

  easy

15 mins

1 hr 30 mins

🍳 **COOK'S TIP**

Other white fish steaks would work equally well and, if you want to push the boat out, try turbot.

This is a rich and flavourful stew of squid, in a sauce of tomatoes and red wine, cooked slowly so that the squid becomes ultra-tender.

Squid Stew

SERVES 4

750 g/1 lb 10 oz squid
3 tbsp olive oil
1 onion, chopped
3 garlic cloves, chopped finely
1 tsp fresh thyme leaves
400 g/14 oz canned chopped tomatoes
150 ml/5 fl oz red wine
300 ml/10 fl oz water
1 tbsp chopped fresh parsley
salt and pepper

to garnish
fresh dill sprigs
lemon slices

1 To prepare whole squid, hold the body firmly and grasp the tentacles just inside the body. Pull firmly to remove the innards. Find the transparent 'backbone' and remove. Grasp the wings on the outside of the body and pull to remove the outer skin. Trim the tentacles just below the beak and reserve. Wash the body and tentacles under cold running water. Slice the body into rings. Drain well on kitchen paper.

2 Heat the olive oil in a large, flameproof casserole over a medium heat. Add the prepared squid and cook, stirring occasionally, until lightly browned.

3 Reduce the heat and add the onion, garlic and thyme. Cook a further 5 minutes until softened.

4 Stir in the tomatoes, red wine and water. Bring to the boil and simmer gently for 2 hours. Stir in the parsley and season to taste with salt and pepper. Transfer to a large, warmed serving dish and garnish with a few sprigs of fresh dill and lemon slices. Serve immediately.

NUTRITION
Calories *284*; Sugars *5 g*; Protein *31 g*;
Carbohydrate *9 g*; Fat *12 g*; Saturates *2 g*

 moderate

20 mins

2 hrs 15 mins

 COOK'S TIP

This dish can be used as the basis of a more substantial stew. Before adding the parsley, add extra seafood such as scallops, pieces of fish or large prawns. Return to the boil and cook for 2 minutes. Add the parsley and seasoning.

This is an impressive-looking Catalan dish using two classic elements of Spanish cooking – the *sofrito*, a slow-cooked mixture of vegetables, and the *picada*, a paste of nuts, bread and garlic used to thicken the stew.

Spanish Fish Stew

1 Heat 3 tablespoons of the olive oil in a frying pan over a low heat. Add the onions and cook for 10–15 minutes until lightly golden, adding a little water to prevent them sticking, if necessary. Add the tomatoes and cook until they are melted down and the oil has separated away from them.

2 Heat 1 tablespoon of the remaining olive oil in a separate frying pan over a medium heat. Add the bread slices and fry until crisp. Break into rough pieces and put into a mortar with the almonds and 2 garlic cloves. Pound with a pestle to make a fine paste. Alternatively, process in a food processor.

3 Split the lobster lengthways. Remove and discard the intestinal vein, which runs down the tail, the stomach sac and the gills. Crack the claws and remove the meat. Remove the flesh from the tail and chop into chunks.

4 Season the monkfish, cod and lobster with salt and pepper and dust with a little flour. Heat a little of the remaining olive oil in a frying pan. Add the fish separately: monkfish, cod, lobster, then the squid, prawns and langoustines and brown, then arrange in a large flameproof casserole.

5 Add the mussels, clams and the remaining garlic and parsley to the casserole. Place over a low heat, then pour over the brandy and ignite. When the flames have died down, add the tomato mixture and just enough water to cover. Bring to the boil and simmer for 3–4 minutes until the mussels and clams have opened. Discard any that remain closed. Stir in the bread and season to taste with salt and pepper. Simmer for a further 5 minutes until all the fish is tender. Transfer to 6 serving plates and garnish with lemon. Serve.

SERVES 6

5 tbsp olive oil
2 large onions, chopped finely
2 ripe tomatoes, peeled, deseeded and diced
2 slices white bread, crusts removed
4 almonds, toasted
3 garlic cloves, chopped roughly
350 g/12 oz cooked lobster
200 g/7 oz monkfish fillet
200 g/7 oz cod fillet, skinned
200 g/7 oz cleaned squid (see page 70), cut into rings
1 tbsp plain flour
6 large raw prawns
6 langoustines
18 live mussels, scrubbed, beards removed
8 large live clams, scrubbed
1 tbsp chopped fresh parsley
125 ml/4 fl oz brandy
salt and pepper
lemon slices, to garnish

NUTRITION
Calories *346*; Sugars *4 g*; Protein *37 g*;
Carbohydrate *11 g*; Fat *13 g*; Saturates *2 g*

 challenging

 30 mins

1 hr

Like all Thai curries, this one has as its base a paste of chillies and spices and a sauce of coconut milk. If you have access to a Thai supplier, buy the curry paste ready-made as the Thais do.

Red Prawn Curry

SERVES 4

2 tbsp vegetable oil
1 garlic clove, chopped finely
1 tbsp red curry paste
200 ml/7 fl oz coconut milk
2 tbsp Thai fish sauce
1 tsp sugar
12 large raw prawns, peeled and deveined
2 kaffir lime leaves, shredded finely
1 fresh red chilli, deseeded and finely sliced
10 leaves fresh Thai basil,
    plus extra to garnish

red curry paste

3 dried long red chillies
½ tsp ground coriander
¼ tsp ground cumin
½ tsp pepper
2 garlic cloves, chopped
2 stalks lemon grass, chopped
1 kaffir lime leaf, chopped finely
1 tsp freshly grated root ginger or galangal
1 tsp shrimp paste, optional
½ tsp salt

NUTRITION

Calories *149*; Sugars *4 g*; Protein *15 g*;
Carbohydrate *6 g*; Fat *7 g*; Saturates *1 g*

        easy

        15 mins

        10 mins

1 Make the red curry paste. Put all the ingredients into a blender or spice grinder and process to a smooth paste, adding a little water, if necessary. Alternatively, pound the ingredients using a mortar and pestle until smooth. Transfer to a bowl and reserve.

2 Heat the vegetable oil in a preheated wok or frying pan over a medium heat until almost smoking. Add the chopped garlic and fry until golden. Add 1 tablespoon of the red curry paste and cook for a further 1 minute. Add half the coconut milk, the Thai fish sauce and the sugar. Stir well. The mixture should thicken slightly.

3 Add the prawns and simmer for 3–4 minutes until they turn pink. Add the remaining coconut milk, the lime leaves and the sliced chilli. Cook for a further 2–3 minutes until the prawns are just tender.

4 Add the basil leaves, stir until wilted and transfer to a large serving dish. Garnish with Thai basil and serve immediately.

⊛ COOK'S TIP

This recipe makes a little more curry paste than you need, but the paste keeps well. Stir a little into canned tuna with some chopped spring onion, lime juice and pinto beans for a delicious sandwich filling.

The best way to approach this recipe is to prepare everything beforehand – including measuring out the spices. The cooking time is then very quick.

Curried Prawns *with* Courgettes

1 Cut the courgettes into small batons, then put into a colander and sprinkle with a little of the salt. Leave to stand for 30 minutes. Rinse, drain and pat dry with kitchen paper. Spread the prawns on kitchen paper to drain.

2 Heat the vegetable oil in a preheated wok or large frying pan over a high heat. Add the garlic. As soon as the garlic begins to brown, add the courgettes, coriander, green chilli, turmeric, cumin, cayenne, tomatoes, ginger, lemon juice and remaining salt. Stir well and bring to the boil.

3 Reduce the heat to low, cover and simmer for about 5 minutes. Uncover and add the prawns.

4 Increase the heat to high and simmer for about 5 minutes to reduce the liquid to a thick sauce. Transfer to 4 large, warmed serving plates and garnish with lime slices. Serve immediately with steamed basmati rice.

SERVES 4

350 g/12 oz small courgettes
1 tsp salt
450 g/1 lb cooked tiger prawns
5 tbsp vegetable oil
4 garlic cloves, chopped finely
5 tbsp chopped fresh coriander
1 fresh green chilli, deseeded and
  finely chopped
½ tsp ground turmeric
1½ tsp ground cumin
pinch of cayenne pepper
200 g/7 oz canned chopped tomatoes
1 tsp freshly grated ginger
1 tbsp lemon juice
lime slices, to garnish
steamed basmati rice, to serve

NUTRITION
Calories 272; Sugars 5 g; Protein 29 g;
Carbohydrate 5 g; Fat 15 g; Saturates 2 g

 easy

40 mins

15 mins

 COOK'S TIP

If you can't find cooked tiger prawns for this recipe, use cooked peeled prawns instead, but these release quite a lot of liquid so you may need to increase the final simmering time to thicken the sauce.

Salads *and* Summer Dishes

Fish is the perfect supper ingredient if you are short of time because it cooks so quickly. It can be marinated and simply grilled or barbecued to make the basis of salads, both warm and cold.

This chapter contains a variety of simple recipes which will taste as if you have spent hours preparing them. There are substantial main course salads, like Tuna Bean Salad, Moroccan Couscous Salad or Caesar Salad.

Quick suppers include the best Cod & Chips ever, plus Salmon Frittata and Tuna Fish Cakes. There are lots of barbecue ideas as well, including Barbecued Monkfish, Chargrilled Scallops and Mixed Seafood Brochettes.

Caesar salad was the invention of a chef at a large hotel in Acapulco in Mexico. This dish has rightly earned an international reputation.

Caesar Salad

SERVES 4

1 large cos lettuce or 2 hearts of romaine
4 canned anchovy fillets, drained and halved lengthways
fresh Parmesan shavings, to garnish

dressing

2 garlic cloves, crushed
1½ tsp Dijon mustard
1 tsp Worcestershire sauce
4 canned anchovy fillets in olive oil, drained and chopped
1 egg yolk
1 tbsp lemon juice
150 ml/5 fl oz olive oil
4 tbsp freshly grated Parmesan cheese
salt and pepper

croûtons

4 thick slices day-old bread
2 tbsp olive oil
1 garlic clove, crushed

NUTRITION

Calories *589*; Sugars *3 g*; Protein *11 g*;
Carbohydrate *24 g*; Fat *50 g*; Saturates *9 g*

 easy

 25 mins

 15–20 mins

1 To make the dressing, put the garlic, mustard, Worcestershire sauce, anchovies, egg yolk, lemon juice and salt and pepper to taste into a food processor or blender and process for 30 seconds until foaming. Keeping the machine running, gradually add the olive oil, drop by drop until the mixture begins to thicken. Continue adding the olive oil in a steady stream until all the oil is incorporated. Transfer the dressing to a small bowl and add a little hot water if the dressing is too thick. Stir in the grated Parmesan cheese. Season to taste with salt and pepper, if necessary, and leave to chill in the refrigerator until required.

2 To make the croûtons, cut the bread into 1-cm/½-inch cubes. Put the olive oil and garlic into a bowl, add the bread cubes and toss well. Arrange on a baking sheet in a single layer and bake in a preheated oven, 180°C/350°F/Gas Mark 4, for 15–20 minutes, stirring occasionally, until the croûtons are browned and crisp. Remove from the oven and leave to cool. Reserve.

3 Separate the cos lettuce into individual leaves and wash. Tear into pieces and spin dry in a salad spinner. Alternatively, dry the leaves on clean kitchen paper. (Excess moisture will dilute the dressing and make the salad taste watery.) Transfer to a polythene bag and leave to chill until required.

4 To assemble the salad, put the lettuce pieces into a large serving bowl. Add the dressing and toss thoroughly until all the leaves are coated. Top with the halved anchovies, croûtons and Parmesan shavings and serve.

Couscous is a type of fine semolina made from wheat. Traditionally it is steamed over a stew in a couscousier, which is a pot with a steamer attachment that sits on top. Nowadays, you can buy precooked couscous, which just needs boiling water.

Moroccan Couscous Salad

1 Cook the couscous according to the packet instructions, omitting any butter recommended. Transfer to a large bowl and reserve.

2 Heat a small frying pan over a high heat. Add the cinnamon stick, coriander seeds and cumin seeds and cook until the seeds begin to pop and smell fragrant. Remove from the heat and pour the seeds into a mortar. Grind with a pestle to a fine powder. Alternatively, grind in a spice grinder. Reserve.

3 Heat the olive oil in a clean frying pan over a low heat. Add the onion and cook for 7–8 minutes until softened and lightly browned. Add the garlic and cook for a further 1 minute. Stir in the roasted and ground spices, turmeric and cayenne and cook for a further 1 minute. Remove from the heat and stir in the lemon juice. Add this mixture to the couscous and mix well, ensuring that all of the grains are coated.

4 Add the sultanas, tomatoes, cucumber, spring onions, tuna and chopped coriander. Season to taste with salt and pepper and mix together. Leave to cool completely and serve at room temperature.

SERVES 4

225 g/8 oz couscous
1 cinnamon stick, about 5 cm/2 inches
2 tsp coriander seeds
1 tsp cumin seeds
2 tbsp olive oil
1 small onion, chopped finely
2 garlic cloves, chopped finely
½ tsp ground turmeric
pinch of cayenne pepper
1 tbsp lemon juice
50 g/1¾ oz sultanas
3 ripe plum tomatoes, chopped
85 g/3 oz cucumber, chopped
4 spring onions, sliced
200 g/7 oz canned tuna in olive oil, drained and flaked
3 tbsp chopped fresh coriander
salt and pepper

NUTRITION
Calories 329; Sugars 12 g; Protein 19 g; Carbohydrate 42 g; Fat 11 g; Saturates 2 g

easy

40 mins

20 mins

🍲 COOK'S TIP
Freshly cooked flaked salmon or tuna would work very well in this salad.

This is a classic version of the French Salade Niçoise. It is a substantial salad, suitable for a lunch or light summer supper.

Tuna Niçoise Salad

SERVES 4

4 eggs
450 g/1 lb new potatoes
115 g/4 oz dwarf green beans, trimmed and halved
2 tuna steaks, about 175 g/6 oz each
6 tbsp olive oil, plus extra for brushing
1 garlic clove, crushed
1½ tsp Dijon mustard
2 tsp lemon juice
2 tbsp chopped fresh basil
2 Little Gem lettuces
200 g/7 oz cherry tomatoes, halved
175 g/6 oz cucumber, peeled, cut in half and sliced
50 g/1¾ oz stoned black olives
50 g/1¾ oz canned anchovy fillets in oil, drained
salt and pepper

NUTRITION
Calories *109*; Sugars *1.1 g*; Protein *7.2 g*; Carbohydrate *4.8 g*; Fat *7 g*; Saturates *1.2 g*

  easy
  10 mins
  20 mins

1 Bring a small saucepan of water to the boil over a medium heat. Add the eggs and cook for 7–9 minutes from when the water returns to the boil – 7 minutes for a slightly soft centre, 9 minutes for a firm centre. Drain and refresh under cold running water. Reserve.

2 Bring a large saucepan of lightly salted water to the boil over a medium heat. Add the potatoes and cook for 10–12 minutes until tender. Add the green beans 3 minutes before the end of the cooking time. Drain both vegetables well and refresh under cold running water. Drain well.

3 Wash the tuna steaks under cold running water and pat dry with kitchen paper. Brush with a little olive oil and season to taste with salt and pepper. Cook on a preheated hot ridged griddle pan for 2–3 minutes each side, until just tender but still slightly pink in the centre. Leave to rest.

4 Whisk the garlic, mustard, lemon juice, basil and seasoning together in a small bowl. Whisk in the olive oil.

5 To assemble the salad, break apart the lettuces and tear into large pieces. Divide between 4 serving plates. Add the potatoes and beans, tomatoes, cucumber and olives. Toss lightly together. Shell the eggs and cut into quarters lengthways. Arrange these on top of the salad. Scatter over the drained anchovies.

6 Flake the tuna steaks and arrange on the salads. Pour over the dressing and serve immediately.

Don't panic if you forget to soak the dried beans overnight. Place them in a saucepan with plenty of water, bring to the boil, turn off the heat and leave to soak, covered, for at least 2 hours before cooking.

Tuna Bean Salad

1 Soak the haricot beans for 8 hours or overnight in at least twice their volume of cold water.

2 When you're ready to cook, drain the beans and place in a saucepan with twice their volume of fresh water. Bring slowly to the boil over a medium heat, skimming off any scum that rises to the surface with a slotted spoon. Boil the beans rapidly for 10 minutes, then reduce the heat and simmer for a further 1¼–1½ hours until the beans are tender.

3 Meanwhile, mix the lemon juice, olive oil, garlic and seasoning together. Drain the beans thoroughly and mix together with the olive oil mixture, onion and parsley. Season to taste with salt and pepper and reserve.

4 Wash the tuna steaks under cold running water and pat dry with kitchen paper. Brush lightly with olive oil and season to taste with salt and pepper. Cook on a preheated ridged griddle pan for 2 minutes on each side until just pink in the centre.

5 Divide the bean salad between 4 serving plates. Top each with a tuna steak. Garnish with a few sprigs of fresh parsley and lemon wedges and serve.

COOK'S TIP

You could use canned haricot beans instead of dried. Reheat according to the instructions on the can, drain and toss with the dressing as above.

SERVES 4

225 g/8 oz dried haricot beans
1 tbsp lemon juice
5 tbsp extra virgin olive oil, plus extra for brushing
1 garlic clove, chopped finely
1 small red onion, very finely sliced (optional)
1 tbsp chopped fresh parsley
4 tuna steaks, about 175 g/6 oz each
salt and pepper

to garnish
fresh flat-leaved parsley sprigs
lemon wedges

NUTRITION
Calories 529; Sugars 3 g; Protein 54 g; Carbohydrate 29 g; Fat 23 g; Saturates 4 g

 easy

8 hrs 15 mins

 1 hr 30 mins

This colourful, refreshing first course is perfect for a special occasion. The dressing can be made in advance and spooned over just before serving.

Warm Tuna Salad

SERVES 4

55 g/2 oz Chinese leaves, shredded
3 tbsp Chinese rice wine
2 tbsp Thai fish sauce
1 tbsp finely shredded fresh root ginger
1 garlic clove, chopped finely
½ small, fresh red bird's-eye chilli, chopped finely
2 tsp soft light brown sugar
2 tbsp lime juice
400 g/14 oz fresh tuna steak
1 tbsp sunflower oil, for brushing
125 g/4½ oz cherry tomatoes
chopped fresh mint leaves and fresh mint sprigs, to garnish

1 Place a small pile of shredded Chinese leaves on a large serving plate. Place the Chinese rice wine, Thai fish sauce, ginger, garlic, chilli, brown sugar and 1 tablespoon of the lime juice in a screw-top jar and shake well to mix.

2 Cut the tuna into strips of an even thickness, then sprinkle with the remaining lime juice.

3 Brush a wide frying pan or ridged griddle pan with the sunflower oil and heat until very hot. Arrange the tuna strips in the pan and cook until just firm and light golden, turning them over once. Remove and reserve.

4 Add the tomatoes to the pan and cook over a high heat until lightly browned. Spoon the tuna and tomatoes over the Chinese leaves and spoon over the dressing. Garnish with chopped fresh mint and mint sprigs and serve warm.

NUTRITION
Calories 177; Sugars 4 g; Protein 13 g; Carbohydrate 6 g; Fat 6 g; Saturates 1 g

 easy

15 mins

8 mins

🍳 **COOK'S TIP**

You can make a quick version of this dish using canned tuna. Just drain and flake the tuna, omit Steps 2 and 3 and continue as in the recipe above.

This unusual seafood dish with a sweet lime dressing can be doubled up for a buffet-style main dish and is a good dish to prepare for a crowd.

Sweet *and* Sour Seafood

1 Clean the mussels by scrubbing or scraping the shells and pulling out any 'beards' that are attached to them. Discard any with broken shells or any that refuse to close when tapped. Put them into a large saucepan with just the water that clings to their shells and cook, covered, over a high heat for about 3–4 minutes, shaking the pan occasionally, until the mussels are opened. Discard any mussels that remain closed. Strain the mussels, reserving the liquid in the pan.

2 Separate the corals from the scallops and cut the whites in half horizontally. Cut the tentacles from the squid and slice the body cavities into rings.

3 Add the shallots to the liquid in the pan and cook over a high heat until the liquid is reduced to about 3 tablespoons. Add the scallops, squid and tiger prawns and stir for 2–3 minutes until cooked. Remove the pan from the heat and spoon the mixture into a wide bowl.

4 Cut the cucumber and carrot in half lengthways, then slice thinly on a diagonal angle to make long, pointed slices. Toss with the Chinese leaves.

5 To make the dressing, place all the ingredients in a screw-top jar and shake well until evenly combined. Season with salt to taste.

6 Toss the vegetables and seafood together. Spoon the dressing over the vegetables and seafood and serve immediately.

SERVES 4

18 live mussels
6 large scallops
200 g/7 oz baby squid, cleaned
2 shallots, chopped finely
6 raw tiger prawns, peeled and deveined
¼ cucumber
1 carrot, peeled
¼ head Chinese leaves, shredded

dressing
4 tbsp lime juice
2 garlic cloves, chopped finely
2 tbsp Thai fish sauce
1 tsp sesame oil
1 tbsp soft light brown sugar
2 tbsp chopped fresh mint
¼ tsp pepper
salt

NUTRITION
Calories *97*; Sugars *5 g*; Protein *13 g*;
Carbohydrate *8 g*; Fat *2 g*; Saturates *0 g*

 moderate

 20 mins

10 mins

Use whatever shellfish is available for this dish. For best results, this salad should be served very cold.

Thai Seafood Salad

SERVES 4

450 g/1 lb live mussels
8 raw tiger prawns
350 g/12 oz squid, cleaned and sliced widthways into rings
115 g/4 oz cooked peeled prawns
½ red onion, sliced finely
½ red pepper, deseeded and finely sliced
115 g/4 oz beansprouts
115 g/4 oz shredded pak choi

dressing

1 garlic clove, crushed
1 tsp grated fresh root ginger
1 fresh red chilli, deseeded and finely chopped
2 tbsp chopped fresh coriander
1 tbsp lime juice
1 tsp finely grated lime rind
1 tbsp light soy sauce
5 tbsp sunflower or groundnut oil
2 tsp sesame oil
4 tbsp cold water
salt and pepper

NUTRITION

Calories *310*; Sugars *4 g*; Protein *30 g*; Carbohydrate *7 g*; Fat *18 g*; Saturates *3 g*

 easy

 1 hr 15 mins

10 mins

1 Clean the mussels by scrubbing or scraping the shells and pulling out any 'beards' that are attached to them. Discard any with broken shells or any that refuse to close when tapped. Put the mussels into a large saucepan with just the water that clings to their shells and cook, covered, over a high heat for 3–4 minutes, shaking the pan occasionally, until all the mussels have opened. Discard any mussels that remain closed. Strain the mussels, reserving the liquid in the pan, and refresh the mussels under cold running water. Drain again and reserve.

2 Bring the reserved liquid to the boil over a medium heat. Add the tiger prawns and simmer for 5 minutes. Add the squid and cook for a further 2 minutes until the prawns and squid are cooked through. Remove them with a slotted spoon and plunge immediately into a large bowl of cold water. Reserve the liquid in the pan. Drain the prawns and squid again.

3 Remove the mussels from their shells and put into a bowl with the tiger prawns, squid and cooked peeled prawns. Leave to chill for 1 hour.

4 To make the dressing, put all the ingredients, except the oils, into a blender or spice grinder and process to a smooth paste. Add the oils, reserved poaching liquid, seasoning to taste and water. Process until blended.

5 Just before serving, mix the onion, red pepper, beansprouts and pak choi in a bowl and toss with 2–3 tablespoons of the dressing. Arrange the vegetables on a large serving plate or in a bowl. Toss the remaining dressing with the seafood to coat and add to the vegetables. Serve immediately.

Noodles and beansprouts form the basis of this refreshing salad, which combines the flavours of fruit and prawns.

Chinese Prawn Salad

1 Place the egg noodles in a large bowl and pour over enough boiling water to cover. Leave to stand for 10 minutes.

2 Drain the noodles thoroughly and pat dry with kitchen paper.

3 Heat the sunflower oil in a large preheated wok or frying pan over a medium heat. Add the noodles and stir-fry for 5 minutes, tossing frequently.

4 Remove the wok from the heat and add the sesame oil, sesame seeds and beansprouts, tossing to mix well.

5 Mix the sliced mango, spring onions, radish and prawns together in a separate bowl. Stir in the soy sauce and sherry and mix until the ingredients are thoroughly blended.

6 Toss the prawn mixture with the noodles and transfer to a large serving dish. Alternatively, arrange the noodles around the edge of a serving plate and pile the prawn mixture in the centre. Serve immediately as this salad is best eaten warm.

SERVES 4

250 g/9 oz fine egg noodles
3 tbsp sunflower oil
1 tbsp sesame oil
1 tbsp sesame seeds
150 g/5½ oz beansprouts
1 ripe mango, sliced
6 spring onions, sliced
75 g/2¾ oz radishes, sliced
350 g/12 oz cooked peeled prawns
2 tbsp light soy sauce
1 tbsp sherry

NUTRITION
Calories *359*; Sugars *4 g*; Protein *31 g*;
Carbohydrate *25 g*; Fat *15 g*; Saturates *2 g*

 easy

 15 mins

5 mins

🧑‍🍳 **COOK'S TIP**

If fresh ripe mangoes are unavailable, use canned mango slices, rinsed and drained, instead.

This salad makes a filling main course or would serve six as a starter. Fresh skate should have a faint smell of ammonia; if the smell is very strong, do not use the fish.

Skate *and* Spinach Salad

SERVES 4

700 g/1 lb 9 oz skate wings, trimmed
2 fresh rosemary sprigs
1 fresh bay leaf
1 tbsp black peppercorns
1 lemon, quartered
450 g/1 lb baby spinach leaves
1 tbsp olive oil
1 small red onion, sliced thinly
2 garlic cloves, crushed
½ tsp crushed chillies
50 g/1¾ oz pine kernels, toasted lightly
50 g/1¾ oz raisins
1 tbsp light muscovado sugar
salt and pepper
2 tbsp chopped fresh parsley, to garnish

NUTRITION
Calories *316*; Sugars *18 g*; Protein *32 g*;
Carbohydrate *18 g*; Fat *13 g*; Saturates *1 g*

   easy

   30 mins

   15 mins

1 Put the skate wings into a large saucepan with the rosemary, bay leaf, peppercorns and lemon quarters. Cover with cold water and bring to the boil over a medium heat. Simmer, covered, for 4–5 minutes until the flesh begins to come away from the cartilage. Remove from the heat and leave to stand for 15 minutes.

2 Lift the fish from the poaching water and remove the flesh from the fish in shreds. Reserve.

3 Meanwhile, put the spinach into a clean saucepan and cook with just the water that clings to its leaves after washing over a high heat for 30 seconds until just wilted. Drain, refresh under cold running water and drain well again. Squeeze out any excess water and reserve.

4 Heat the olive oil in a large, deep frying pan over a low heat. Add the red onion and fry for 3–4 minutes until softened, but not browned. Add the garlic, crushed chillies, pine kernels, raisins and sugar. Cook for 1–2 minutes, then add the spinach and toss for 1 minute until heated through.

5 Gently fold in the skate and cook for a further 1 minute. Season well with salt and pepper.

6 Divide the salad between 4 serving plates and garnish with the chopped parsley. Serve immediately.

A colourful combination of cooked mussels tossed together with chargrilled red peppers, radicchio and rocket, and a lemon and chive dressing. It makes a delicious main meal.

Mussel *and* Red Pepper Salad

1 Halve and deseed the peppers and place them skin side up on a grill rack. Cook under a preheated hot grill for 8–10 minutes until the skin is charred and blistered and the flesh is soft. Leave to cool for 10 minutes, then peel off the skin.

2 Slice the pepper flesh into thin strips and place in a bowl. Gently mix in the shelled mussels and reserve.

3 To make the dressing, mix all of the ingredients in a small bowl until well blended. Mix into the pepper and mussel mixture until coated.

4 Remove the central core of the radicchio and shred the leaves. Place in a serving bowl with the rocket leaves and toss together.

5 Pile the mussel mixture into the centre of the leaves and arrange the large mussels around the edge of the dish. Garnish with strips of lemon rind and serve immediately with crusty bread.

SERVES 4

2 large red peppers
350 g/12 oz cooked shelled mussels, thawed if frozen
1 head of radicchio
25 g/1 oz rocket leaves
8 cooked New Zealand mussels in their shells
strips of lemon rind, to garnish
crusty bread, to serve

dressing
1 tbsp olive oil
1 tbsp lemon juice
1 tsp finely grated lemon rind
2 tsp clear honey
1 tsp French mustard
1 tbsp snipped fresh chives
salt and pepper

NUTRITION
Calories *180*; Sugars *10 g*; Protein *18 g*; Carbohydrate *14 g*; Fat *6 g*; Saturates *1 g*

  easy / 30 mins / 10 mins

COOK'S TIP

Replace the shelled mussels with peeled prawns and the New Zealand mussels with large crevettes, if you prefer. Lime could be used instead of lemon for a different citrus flavour.

Try to get small red mullet for this dish. If you can only get larger fish, serve one to each person and then increase the cooking time accordingly.

Grilled Red Mullet

SERVES 4

1 lemon, sliced thinly
2 garlic cloves, crushed
4 fresh flat-leaved parsley sprigs
4 fresh thyme sprigs
8 fresh sage leaves
2 large shallots, sliced
8 small red mullet, cleaned
8 slices Parma ham
salt and pepper

sauté potatoes and shallots

4 tbsp olive oil
900 g/2 lb potatoes, diced
8 whole garlic cloves, unpeeled
12 small whole shallots

dressing

4 tbsp olive oil
1 tbsp lemon juice
1 tbsp chopped fresh flat-leaved parsley
1 tbsp snipped fresh chives

NUTRITION

Calories *111*; Sugars *0.8 g*; Protein *10.2 g*;
Carbohydrate *6 g*; Fat *5 g*; Saturates *1 g*

  moderate

10 mins

20 mins

1 For the sauté potatoes and shallots, heat the olive oil in a large frying pan over a medium heat. Add the potatoes, garlic cloves and shallots and cook gently, stirring regularly, for 12–15 minutes until golden, crisp and tender.

2 Meanwhile, divide the lemon slices, halved if necessary, garlic, parsley, thyme, sage and shallots between the cavities of the fish. Season well with salt and pepper. Wrap a slice of Parma ham around each fish and secure with a cocktail stick .

3 Arrange the fish on a grill pan and cook under a preheated hot grill for about 5–6 minutes on each side until tender.

4 To make the dressing, mix the olive oil and lemon juice, parsley and chives together in a small bowl. Season to taste with salt and pepper.

5 Divide the potatoes and shallots between 4 large serving plates and top each with the fish. Drizzle around the dressing and serve immediately.

Liven up firm steaks of white fish with a spicy, colourful relish. Use red onions for a slightly sweeter flavour.

Pan-seared Halibut

1 To make the relish, shred the onions and shallots thinly, then place in a small bowl and toss in the lemon juice.

2 Heat the olive oil for the relish in a frying pan over a medium heat. Add the onions and shallots and fry for 3–4 minutes until just softened.

3 Add the vinegar and sugar and continue to cook for a further 2 minutes over a high heat. Pour in the stock and season well with salt and pepper. Bring to the boil and simmer gently for a further 8–9 minutes until the sauce has thickened and is slightly reduced.

4 Brush a non-stick, ridged griddle pan or frying pan with olive oil and heat over a medium–high heat until hot. Press the fish into the pan to seal, reduce the heat and cook for 4 minutes. Turn the fish over and cook for 4–5 minutes until cooked through. Drain on kitchen paper and keep warm.

5 Stir the cornflour paste into the onion relish and heat through, stirring, until thickened. Season to taste with salt and pepper.

6 Pile the relish on to 4 warmed serving plates and place a halibut steak on top of each. Garnish with snipped chives and serve.

SERVES 4

1 tsp olive oil
4 halibut steaks, skinned, about
     175 g/6 oz each
½ tsp cornflour mixed with 2 tsp cold water
salt and pepper
2 tbsp snipped fresh chives, to garnish

red onion relish

2 medium red onions
6 shallots
1 tbsp lemon juice
2 tsp olive oil
2 tbsp red wine vinegar
2 tsp caster sugar
150 ml/5 fl oz fish stock

 COOK'S TIP

If raw onions make your eyes water, try peeling them under cold running water. Alternatively, stand or sit well back from the onion so that your face isn't directly over it.

NUTRITION
Calories *197*; Sugars *1 g*; Protein *31 g*;
Carbohydrate *2 g*; Fat *7 g*; Saturates *1 g*

⭐⭐⭐   moderate

🕐   55 mins

🕐   30 mins

This is a wonderful dish to serve as part of a buffet lunch or supper and can be eaten hot or cold.

Baked Salmon

SERVES 8–10

3 kg/6 lb 8 oz salmon, filleted
8 tbsp chopped mixed herbs
2 tbsp green peppercorns in brine, drained
1 tsp finely grated lime rind
6 tbsp dry vermouth or dry white wine
salt and pepper
fresh parsley sprigs, to garnish

red pepper relish

125 ml/4 fl oz white wine vinegar
300 ml/10 fl oz light olive oil
1–2 tsp chilli sauce, to taste
6 spring onions, sliced finely
1 orange or red pepper, deseeded and diced
1 tbsp chopped fresh flat-leaved parsley
2 tbsp snipped fresh chives

caper and gherkin mayonnaise

350 ml/12 fl oz good-quality mayonnaise
3 tbsp chopped capers
3 tbsp finely chopped gherkins
2 tbsp chopped fresh flat-leaved parsley
1 tbsp Dijon mustard

NUTRITION
Calories *892*; Sugars *2 g*; Protein *41 g*;
Carbohydrate *2 g*; Fat *79 g*; Saturates *12 g*

 easy

30 mins

12 mins

1 Wash the salmon fillets under cold running water and pat dry with kitchen paper. Place 1 fillet, skin side down, on a large sheet of oiled foil. Mix the herbs, peppercorns and lime rind together and spread over the top. Season well with salt and pepper and lay the second fillet on top, skin side up. Drizzle over the vermouth or white wine. Wrap the foil over the salmon, twisting well to make a loose but tightly sealed parcel.

2 Transfer the foil parcel to a large baking sheet and bake in a preheated oven, 120/C°250°F/Gas Mark ½, for 1½ hours until tender. Remove from the oven and leave to rest for 20 minutes before serving.

3 Meanwhile, make the red pepper relish. Whisk the vinegar, olive oil and chilli sauce together in a small bowl. Add the spring onions, pepper, parsley and chives. Season to taste with salt and pepper and reserve.

4 To make the caper and gherkin mayonnaise, mix all the ingredients together in a small bowl and reserve.

5 Unwrap the cooked salmon and slice thickly. Arrange the slices on a large serving plate and garnish with fresh parsley sprigs. Serve with the red pepper relish and caper and gherkin mayonnaise.

Monkfish cooks very well on a lit barbecue because it is a firm-fleshed fish.

Barbecued Monkfish

1 Mix the olive oil, lime rind, Thai fish sauce, garlic, ginger and basil together. Season to taste with salt and pepper and reserve.

2 Wash the fish under a cold running water and pat dry with kitchen paper. Add to the marinade and mix well. Cover and leave to marinate in the refrigerator for 2 hours, stirring occasionally.

3 If using bamboo skewers, soak them in cold water for 30 minutes. Then, lift the monkfish pieces from the marinade and thread them on to the skewers, alternating with the lime wedges.

4 Transfer the skewers, either to a lit barbecue or to a preheated ridged griddle pan and cook for 5–6 minutes, turning regularly, until the fish is tender. Pile freshly cooked noodles on to 4 large serving plates and put the monkfish skewers on top. Garnish with a few fresh basil leaves and serve.

SERVES 4

4 tbsp olive oil
grated rind of 1 lime
2 tsp Thai fish sauce
2 garlic cloves, crushed
1 tsp grated fresh root ginger
2 tbsp chopped fresh basil
700 g/1 lb 9 oz monkfish fillet, cut into chunks
2 limes, each cut into 6 wedges
salt and pepper
fresh basil leaves, to garnish
freshly cooked noodles, to serve

NUTRITION
Calories 219; Sugars 2 g; Protein 41 g; Carbohydrate 2 g; Fat 79 g; Saturates 12 g

easy

2 hrs 10 mins
1 hr 30 mins

🧑‍🍳 **COOK'S TIP**

You could use any type of white fleshed fish for this recipe, but sprinkle the pieces with salt and leave for 2 hours to firm the flesh, before rinsing, drying and then adding to the marinade.

Tuna has a firm flesh, which is ideal for barbecuing, but it can be a little dry unless it is marinated first.

Charred Tuna Steaks

SERVES 4

4 tuna steaks
3 tbsp soy sauce
1 tbsp Worcestershire sauce
1 tsp wholegrain mustard
1 tsp caster sugar
1 tbsp sunflower oil
green salad, to serve

to garnish
fresh flat-leaved parsley sprigs
lemon wedges

1 Place the tuna steaks in a large, shallow dish.

2 Mix the soy sauce, Worcestershire sauce, mustard, sugar and sunflower oil together in a small bowl. Pour the marinade over the tuna steaks.

3 Gently turn over the tuna steaks, using your fingers or a fork, so that they are well coated with the marinade.

4 Cover with clingfilm and leave the tuna steaks to marinate in the refrigerator for at least 30 minutes or preferably 2 hours.

5 Transfer the marinated fish to a lit barbecue and cook over hot coals for 10–15 minutes, turning once. Baste frequently with any of the marinade that is left in the dish.

6 Transfer the tuna to 4 large serving plates, garnish with parsley sprigs and lemon wedges and serve with a green salad.

NUTRITION
Calories *510*; Sugars *38 g*; Protein *33 g*; Carbohydrate *44 g*; Fat *24 g*; Saturates *11 g*

 moderate

 2 hrs

15 mins

COOK'S TIP

If a marinade contains soy sauce, the marinating time should be limited, usually to 2 hours. If allowed to marinate for too long, the fish will dry out and become tough.

The word 'blackened' refers to the spicy marinade that is used to coat the fish and that chars slightly as it cooks. Choose a fish with a firm texture, such as hake or halibut, for this dish.

Blackened Fish

1 Wash the fish under cold running water and pat dry with kitchen paper.

2 Mix the paprika, thyme, cayenne, black and white peppers, salt and allspice together in a shallow dish.

3 Place the butter and oil in a small saucepan and heat over a low heat, stirring occasionally, until the butter melts.

4 Brush the butter mixture liberally all over the fish steaks on both sides.

5 Dip the fish into the spicy mix until well coated on both sides.

6 Transfer the fish to a lit barbecue and cook over hot coals for 10 minutes on each side, turning once. Continue to baste the fish with the remaining butter mixture during the cooking time. Transfer the fish to 4 large, serving plates and serve with mixed salad leaves.

SERVES **4**

4 white fish steaks
1 tbsp paprika
1 tsp dried thyme
1 tsp cayenne pepper
1 tsp freshly ground black pepper
½ tsp freshly ground white pepper
½ tsp salt
¼ tsp ground allspice
50 g/1¾ oz unsalted butter
3 tbsp sunflower oil
mixed salad leaves, to serve

 COOK'S TIP

A whole fish – red mullet, for example – rather than steaks is also delicious cooked this way. The spicy seasoning can also be used to coat chicken portions, if you prefer.

NUTRITION
Calories *370*; Sugars *0 g*; Protein *27 g*;
Carbohydrate *52 g*; Fat *8 g*; Saturates *1 g*

 moderate

5–10 mins

20 mins

The Japanese sauce used
here combines very well
with salmon, although
it is usually served
with chicken.

Salmon Yakitori

SERVES 4

350 g/12 oz chunky salmon fillet
8 baby leeks
mixed fresh herbs, to garnish

yakitori sauce
5 tbsp light soy sauce
5 tbsp fish stock
2 tbsp caster sugar
5 tbsp dry white wine
3 tbsp sweet sherry
1 garlic clove, crushed

NUTRITION
Calories 247; Sugars 10 g; Protein 19 g;
Carbohydrate 12 g; Fat 11 g; Saturates 2 g

easy

20 mins

15 mins

1 Skin the salmon and cut the flesh into 5-cm/2-inch chunks. Trim the leeks and cut them into 5-cm/2-inch lengths.

2 Thread the salmon and leeks alternately on to 8 presoaked wooden skewers. Leave to chill in the refrigerator until required.

3 To make the sauce, place all of the ingredients in a small saucepan and heat gently over a low heat, stirring, until the sugar dissolves. Bring to the boil, then reduce the heat and simmer for 2 minutes. Strain the sauce and leave to cool. Pour about one third of the sauce into a small dish and reserve to serve with the kebabs.

4 Brush plenty of the remaining sauce over the skewers and transfer the skewers to a lit barbecue. Cook over hot coals for 10 minutes, turning once. Cook directly on a grill rack or, if preferred, place a sheet of oiled foil on the grill rack and cook the salmon on the foil. Baste frequently with the remaining sauce during cooking to prevent the fish and vegetables from drying out.

5 Transfer the kebabs to a large serving plate, garnish with mixed herbs and serve with the reserved sauce for dipping.

COOK'S TIP

Soak wooden skewers in cold water for at least 30 minutes to prevent them burning during cooking. You can make the kebabs and sauce several hours beforehand and keep in the refrigerator until required.

A delicious aromatic coating makes this dish rather special. Serve it with a crisp salad and crusty bread.

Indonesian-style Spicy Cod

1 Wash the cod steaks under cold running water and pat dry on kitchen paper.

2 Remove and discard the outer leaves from the lemon grass and thinly slice the inner section.

3 Place the lemon grass, onion, garlic, chillies, ginger and turmeric in a food processor and process until finely chopped. Season to taste with salt and pepper. Keeping the machine running, add the butter, coconut milk and lemon juice and process until well blended.

4 Place the fish in a shallow, non-metallic dish. Pour over the coconut mixture and turn the fish until well coated.

5 If you have one, place the fish steaks in a hinged basket, which will make them easier to turn. Transfer the fish steaks to a lit barbecue and cook over hot coals for 15 minutes or until the fish is cooked through, turning once. Transfer to 4 large serving plates, garnish with red chillies, if wished and serve with mixed salad leaves.

SERVES 4

4 cod steaks
1 lemon grass stalk
1 small red onion, chopped
3 garlic cloves, chopped
2 fresh red chillies, deseeded and chopped
1 tsp grated fresh root ginger
¼ tsp turmeric
2 tbsp butter, cut into small cubes
8 tbsp canned coconut milk
2 tbsp lemon juice
salt and pepper
fresh red chillies, to garnish (optional)
mixed salad leaves, to serve

NUTRITION
Calories *146*; Sugars *2 g*; Protein *19 g*;
Carbohydrate *2 g*; Fat *7 g*; Saturates *4 g*

 easy

10 mins

 15 mins

COOK'S TIP

If you prefer a milder flavour omit the chillies altogether. For a hotter flavour do not remove the seeds from the chillies.

This is the genuine article. A crunchy, deep golden batter surrounding perfectly cooked fish, served with golden crispy chips. If you've never had chips with mayonnaise, try them with this lovely mustardy version and you'll be converted.

Cod *and* Chips

S E R V E S 4

900 g/2 lb old potatoes
600 ml/1 pint vegetable oil, for deep-frying
4 thick pieces cod fillet, preferably from the
    head end, about 175 g/6 oz each
salt and pepper

b a t t e r
15 g/½ oz fresh yeast
300 ml/10 fl oz beer
225 g/8 oz plain flour
2 tsp salt

m a y o n n a i s e
1 egg yolk
1 tsp wholegrain mustard
1 tbsp lemon juice
200 ml/7 fl oz light olive oil

t o g a r n i s h
lemon wedges
fresh parsley sprigs

N U T R I T I O N

Calories *584*; Sugars *0 g*; Protein *28 g*;
Carbohydrate *1 g*; Fat *48 g*; Saturates *7 g*

  easy

1 hr 10 mins

  30–35 mins

1 To make the batter, cream the yeast with a little of the beer to a smooth paste. Gradually stir in the rest of the beer. Sift the flour and salt into a bowl, make a well in the centre and add the yeast mixture. Gradually whisk to a smooth batter. Cover and leave at room temperature for 1 hour.

2 To make the mayonnaise, put the egg yolk, mustard, lemon juice and seasoning into a food processor. Process for 30 seconds until frothy. Gradually add the olive oil, drop by drop, until the mixture begins to thicken. Continue adding the olive oil in a slow, steady stream until all the oil is incorporated. Season to taste with salt and pepper, if necessary. Add a little hot water if the mayonnaise is too thick. Leave to chill until required.

3 For the chips, cut the potatoes into chips about 1.5-cm/½-inch thick. Half fill a large saucepan with vegetable oil and heat to 140°C/275°F, or until a cube of bread browns in 1 minute. Cook the chips in 2 batches for 5 minutes until cooked through but not browned. Drain on kitchen paper and reserve.

4 Increase the heat to 160°C/325°F, or until a cube of bread browns in 45 seconds. Season the fish with salt and pepper, then dip into the batter. Fry 2 pieces at a time for 7–8 minutes until golden-brown and cooked through. Drain on kitchen paper and keep warm while you cook remaining fish.

5 Increase the heat to 190°C/375°F, or until a cube of bread browns in 30 seconds. Fry the chips again, in 2 batches, for 2–3 minutes until crisp and golden. Drain on kitchen paper and sprinkle with salt. Serve the fish with the chips and mayonnaise, garnished with lemon wedges and parsley sprigs.

The Italian flatbread known as focaccia is what makes these battered haddock fingers taste so special.

Haddock Goujons

1 Put the focaccia into a food processor and process until fine crumbs form. Reserve. Thinly slice the haddock fillet widthways into fingers. Put the flour, egg and breadcrumbs into separate bowls.

2 Dip the haddock fingers into the flour, then the egg and finally the breadcrumbs to coat. Lay on a plate and leave to chill in the refrigerator for 30 minutes.

3 To make the tartare sauce, put the egg yolk, mustard, vinegar and seasoning into a food processor and process for 30 seconds until frothy. Gradually add the olive oil, drop by drop, until the mixture begins to thicken. Continue adding the olive oil in a slow, steady stream until all the oil is incorporated.

4 Transfer the sauce to a small bowl and stir in the olives, gherkins, capers, chives and parsley. Season to taste with salt and pepper, if necessary. Add a little hot water if the sauce is too thick.

5 Half fill a large saucepan with vegetable oil and heat to 190°C/375°F, or until a cube of bread browns in 30 seconds. Add the haddock goujons, in batches of 3 or 4, and cook for 3–4 minutes until the crumbs are browned and crisp and the fish is cooked. Drain on kitchen paper and keep warm while you cook the remaining fish.

6 Transfer the haddock goujons to 4 large serving plates and garnish with lemon wedges and a few sprigs of fresh parsley. Serve immediately with the tartare sauce.

SERVES 4

175 g/6 oz herb focaccia bread
700 g/1 lb 9 oz skinless, boneless
   haddock fillet
2–3 tbsp plain flour
2 eggs, beaten lightly
600 ml/1 pint vegetable oil, for deep-frying

tartare sauce
1 egg yolk
1 tsp Dijon mustard
2 tsp white wine vinegar
150 ml/5 fl oz light olive oil
1 tsp finely chopped green olives
1 tsp finely chopped gherkins
1 tsp finely chopped capers
2 tsp chopped fresh chives
2 tsp chopped fresh parsley
salt and pepper

to garnish
lemon wedges
fresh parsley sprigs

NUTRITION
Calories 762; Sugars 1 g; Protein 9 g;
Carbohydrate 4 g; Fat 10 g; Saturates 0.5 g

 moderate

50 mins

15 mins

The marinade for this dish has a distinctly Japanese flavour. Its subtle taste goes very well with any white fish.

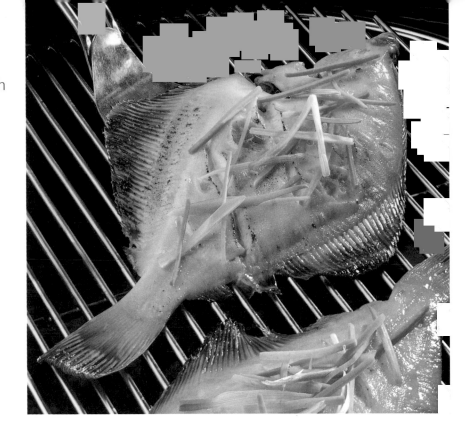

Japanese Plaice

SERVES 4

4 small plaice
6 tbsp soy sauce
2 tbsp sake or dry white wine
2 tbsp sesame oil
1 tbsp lemon juice
2 tbsp light muscovado sugar
1 tsp fresh root ginger, grated
1 garlic clove, crushed

to garnish
1 small carrot
4 spring onions

1 Wash the fish under cold running water and pat dry on kitchen paper.

2 Using a sharp knife, cut a few slashes into the sides of the fish so that they absorb the marinade.

3 Mix the soy sauce, sake or wine, sesame oil, lemon juice, sugar, ginger and garlic together in a large, shallow dish.

4 Place the fish in the marinade and turn them over until the fish is well coated on both sides. Cover and leave to marinate in the refrigerator for about 1–6 hours.

5 Meanwhile, prepare the garnish. Cut the carrot into evenly sized thin sticks and shred the spring onions.

6 Transfer the fish to a lit barbecue and cook over hot coals for 10 minutes, turning once.

7 Scatter the spring onions and carrot over the fish and transfer the fish to a serving dish. Serve immediately.

NUTRITION
Calories *207*; Sugars *9 g*; Protein *22 g*;
Carbohydrate *10 g*; Fat *8 g*; Saturates *1 g*

easy

1 hr 10 mins

10 mins

The cooking time may seem long and indeed you could decrease it slightly if you prefer, but in Morocco they like their fish well cooked!

Hake Steaks *with* Chermoula

1 To make the marinade, mix the fresh coriander, parsley, garlic, cumin, coriander, paprika, cayenne, lemon juice and olive oil together in a bowl.

2 Wash the hake steaks under cold running water and pat dry with kitchen paper. Place in an ovenproof dish and pour over the marinade. Cover with clingfilm and leave to marinate in the refrigerator for at least 1 hour or preferably overnight.

3 Before cooking, scatter the olives over the fish. Cover the dish with foil.

4 Cook in a preheated oven, 160°C/325°F/Gas Mark 3, for 35–40 minutes until the fish is tender. Transfer the fish to 4 large serving plates, garnish with lemon slices and serve with freshly cooked vegetables.

SERVES 4

4 hake steaks, about 225 g/8 oz each
115 g/4 oz stoned green olives
lemon slices, to garnish
freshly cooked vegetables, to serve

marinade
6 tbsp chopped finely fresh coriander
6 tbsp chopped finely fresh parsley
6 garlic cloves, crushed
1 tbsp ground cumin
1 tsp ground coriander
1 tbsp paprika
pinch of cayenne pepper
150 ml/5 fl oz fresh lemon juice
300 ml/10 fl oz olive oil

NUTRITION
Calories *590*; Sugars *1 g*; Protein *42 g*;
Carbohydrate *2 g*; Fat *46 g*; Saturates *7 g*

easy

1 hr 15 mins

35–40 mins

🍳 **COOK'S TIP**

For fried fish, remove the fish from the marinade and dust with seasoned flour. Fry in oil or clarified butter until golden. Warm through the marinade, but do not boil, and serve as a sauce with lemon slices.

This is a variation of a Middle Eastern recipe for stuffed mackerel, which involves removing the mackerel flesh, while leaving the skin intact, and then re-stuffing the skin. This version is much simpler.

Stuffed Mackerel

SERVES 4

4 large mackerel, cleaned
1 tbsp olive oil
1 small onion, sliced finely
1 tsp ground cinnamon
½ ground ginger
2 tbsp raisins
2 tbsp pine kernels, toasted
8 vine leaves in brine, drained
salt and pepper
lemon slices, to garnish

to serve
mixed salad
plain boiled rice

1 Wash the fish under cold running water and pat dry with kitchen paper, then reserve. Heat the olive oil in a small frying pan over a low heat. Add the onion and cook gently for 5 minutes until softened. Add the cinnamon and ginger and cook for 30 seconds before adding the raisins and pine kernels. Remove from the heat and leave to cool.

2 Stuff each of the fish with one-quarter of the stuffing mixture. Wrap each fish in 2 vine leaves, securing with cocktail sticks.

3 Transfer to a lit barbecue or a preheated ridged griddle pan and cook for about 5 minutes on each side until the vine leaves have scorched and the fish is tender. Transfer to 4 large serving plates and garnish with lemon slices. Serve immediately with a mixed salad and plain boiled rice.

NUTRITION
Calories *488*; Sugars *12 g*; Protein *34 g*;
Carbohydrate *12 g*; Fat *34 g*; Saturates *6 g*

  easy

10 mins

20 mins

COOK'S TIP

This stuffing works equally well with many other fish, including sea bass and red mullet.

These fish cakes make a very satisfying and quick mid-week supper.

Tuna Fish Cakes

1 To make the tuna fish cakes, bring a large saucepan of lightly salted water to the boil over a medium heat. Add the potatoes and cook for 12–15 minutes until tender. Drain well, then mash, leaving a few lumps, and reserve.

2 Heat the olive oil in a frying pan over a low heat. Add the shallot and cook for 5 minutes until softened. Add the garlic and thyme and cook for a further 1 minute. Leave to cool slightly, then add to the potatoes with the tuna, lemon rind, parsley and salt and pepper to taste. Mix, but leave texture.

3 Form the mixture into 6–8 cakes. Put the flour, egg and breadcrumbs into separate bowls. Dip the cakes first in the flour, then the egg and finally the breadcrumbs to coat. Lay on a plate and leave to chill for 30 minutes.

4 Meanwhile, make the tomato sauce. Put the olive oil, tomatoes, garlic, sugar, lemon rind, basil and salt and pepper to taste into a saucepan and bring to the boil over a low heat. Cover and simmer gently for 30 minutes. Uncover and simmer for a further 15 minutes until thickened.

5 Heat enough vegetable oil in a frying pan to generously cover the base. When hot, add the fish cakes, in batches, and fry for 3–4 minutes on each side until golden and crisp. Drain on kitchen paper and keep warm while you fry the remaining fish cakes. Serve hot with the tomato sauce.

SERVES 4

225 g/8 oz potatoes, cubed
1 tbsp olive oil
1 large shallot, chopped finely
1 garlic clove, chopped finely
1 tsp thyme leaves
400 g/14 oz canned tuna in olive oil, drained
grated rind ½ lemon
1 tbsp chopped fresh parsley
2–3 tbsp plain flour
1 egg, beaten lightly
115 g/4 oz fresh breadcrumbs
125 ml/4 fl oz vegetable oil, for shallow-frying
salt and pepper

quick tomato sauce
2 tbsp olive oil
400 g/14 oz canned chopped tomatoes
1 garlic clove, crushed
½ tsp sugar
grated rind ½ lemon
1 tbsp chopped fresh basil

NUTRITION
Calories *638*; Sugars *5 g*; Protein *35 g*; Carbohydrate *38 g*; Fat *40 g*; Saturates *5 g*

 moderate

 35 mins

1 hr 15 mins

This is called *Foo Yung* in China and is a classic dish, which may be flavoured with any ingredients you have to hand.

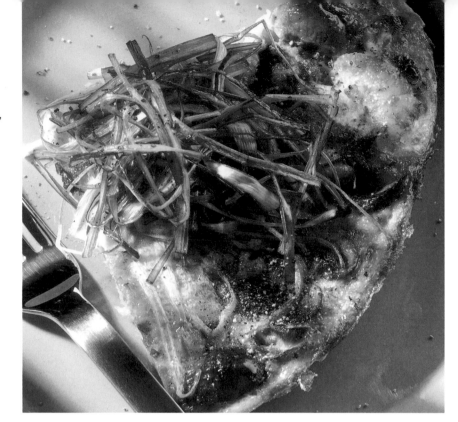

Prawn Omelette

SERVES 4

3 tbsp sunflower oil
2 leeks, sliced
4 tbsp cornflour
1 tsp salt
350 g/12 oz raw tiger prawns, peeled
175 g/6 oz mushrooms, sliced
175 g/6 oz beansprouts
6 eggs
3 tbsp cold water
deep-fried leeks, to garnish (optional)

1 Heat the sunflower oil in a preheated wok or large, heavy-based frying pan over a medium heat. Add the leeks and stir-fry for 3 minutes.

2 Mix the cornflour and salt together in a large bowl.

3 Add the prawns to the cornflour and salt mixture and toss to coat all over.

4 Add the prawns to the wok or frying pan and stir-fry for 2 minutes, or until the prawns have changed colour and are almost cooked through.

5 Add the mushrooms and beansprouts to the wok and stir-fry for a further 2 minutes.

6 Beat the eggs with the water in a small bowl. Pour the egg mixture into the wok and cook until the egg sets, carefully turning the omelette over once. Turn the omelette out on to a clean board, divide into 4 and serve hot, garnished with deep-fried leeks (if using).

NUTRITION
Calories *320*; Sugars *1 g*; Protein *31 g*;
Carbohydrate *8 g*; Fat *18 g*; Saturates *4 g*

 moderate

10 mins

10 mins

🍲 **COOK'S TIP**

If liked, divide the mixture for the filling into 4 at the end of Step 5, and make 4 individual omelettes.

This is a very quick and tasty mid-week supper dish. You could use a good quality ready-made pesto to save more time.

Sardines *with* Pesto

1 Wash the sardines under cold running water and pat dry with kitchen paper. Arrange on a grill pan.

2 Put the basil leaves, garlic and pine kernels into a food processor and process until finely chopped. Transfer to a bowl and stir in the Parmesan cheese and olive oil. Season to taste with salt and pepper.

3 Spread a little of the pesto over one side of the sardines and place under a preheated hot grill for 3 minutes. Turn the fish, spread with more pesto, and grill for a further 3 minutes until the sardines are cooked.

4 Transfer the fish to 4 serving plates, garnish with a few sprigs of fresh dill and lemon wedges. Serve immediately with extra pesto, garnished with strips of lemon rind.

SERVES 4

16 large sardines, scaled and gutted
50 g/1³⁄₄ oz fresh basil leaves
2 garlic cloves, crushed
2 tbsp pine kernels, toasted
50 g/1³⁄₄ oz freshly grated Parmesan cheese
150 ml/5 fl oz olive oil
salt and pepper

to garnish
fresh dill sprigs
lemon wedges
strips of lemon rind

NUTRITION
Calories *617*; Sugars *0 g*; Protein *27 g*;
Carbohydrate *1 g*; Fat *56 g*; Saturates *11 g*

 easy

 25 mins

 6 mins

COOK'S TIP

This treatment will also work well with other small oily fish such as herrings and pilchards.

A frittata is an Italian slow-cooked omelette, not dissimilar to the Spanish tortilla. Here it is filled with poached salmon, fresh herbs and vegetables to make a substantial dish.

Salmon Frittata

SERVES 4

250 g/9 oz skinless, boneless salmon
3 fresh thyme sprigs
1 fresh parsley sprig, plus 2 tbsp chopped
   fresh parsley
5 black peppercorns
½ small onion, sliced
½ celery stick, sliced
½ carrot, chopped
175 g/6 oz asparagus spears, chopped
80 g/3 oz baby carrots, halved
50 g/1¾ oz butter
1 large onion, sliced finely
1 garlic clove, chopped finely
115 g/4 oz peas, fresh or frozen
8 eggs, beaten lightly
1 tbsp chopped fresh dill
salt and pepper

to serve
crème fraîche
salad
lemon wedges
crusty bread

NUTRITION

Calories *300*; Sugars *5 g*; Protein *22 g*;
Carbohydrate *7 g*; Fat *21 g*; Saturates *8 g*

   moderate

🕐   15 mins

🕐   1 hr

1 Place the salmon in a saucepan with a sprig of the thyme, the parsley sprig, peppercorns, onion, celery and carrot. Cover the vegetables and fish with cold water and bring slowly to the boil over a low heat. Remove the pan from the heat and leave to stand for 5 minutes. Lift the fish out of the the poaching liquid, flake the flesh and reserve. Discard the poaching liquid.

2 Bring a saucepan of lightly salted water to the boil over a medium heat. Add the asparagus and blanch for 2 minutes. Drain and refresh under cold running water. Blanch the carrots for 4 minutes. Drain and refresh under cold running water. Drain again and pat dry with kitchen paper. Reserve.

3 Heat half the butter in a large frying pan over a low heat. Add the onion and cook gently for 8–10 minutes until softened, but not coloured. Add the garlic and remaining thyme and cook for a further 1 minute. Add the asparagus, carrots and peas and heat through. Remove the pan from the heat.

4 Add the vegetables to the eggs with the chopped parsley, dill and salmon and season to taste with salt and pepper. Stir briefly. Heat the remaining butter in the pan and return the mixture to the pan. Cover and cook over a low heat for 10 minutes.

5 Transfer the frittata to a grill rack and cook under a preheated medium–hot grill for a further 5 minutes until set and golden. Serve hot or cold in wedges topped with crème fraîche, salad, lemon wedges and crusty bread.

You can use turbot and salmon steaks instead of fillets for these brochettes. Remove the skin and bones yourself and chop the flesh into large chunks.

Mixed Seafood Brochettes

1 Chop the turbot and salmon into 8 pieces each. Thread on to 8 metal skewers, with the scallops and tiger prawns or langoustines, alternating with the bay leaves and lemon slices. Put into a non-metallic dish in a single layer, if possible.

2 Mix the olive oil, lemon rind, herbs and pepper together in a bowl and pour over the fish. Cover and leave to marinate in the refrigerator for 2 hours, turning once or twice.

3 To make the lemon butter rice, bring a large saucepan of lightly salted water to the boil over a medium heat. Add the rice and lemon rind, return to the boil and simmer for about 7–8 minutes until the rice is tender. Drain well and immediately stir in the lemon juice and butter. Season to taste with salt and pepper.

4 Meanwhile, lift the fish brochettes from their marinade and cook on a lit barbecue or under a preheated hot grill for 8–10 minutes, turning regularly, until cooked through. Transfer to 4 large serving plates, garnish with lemon wedges and a few sprigs of fresh dill, and serve with the lemon butter rice.

SERVES 4

225 g/8 oz skinless, boneless turbot fillet
225 g/8 oz skinless, boneless salmon fillet
8 scallops
8 large raw tiger prawns or langoustines
16 bay leaves
1 lemon, sliced
4 tbsp olive oil
grated rind 1 lemon
4 tbsp chopped mixed herbs such as thyme, parsley, chives and basil
salt and pepper

lemon butter rice
175 g/6 oz long-grain rice
grated rind and juice 1 lemon
50 g/1¾ oz butter

to garnish
lemon wedges
fresh dill sprigs

NUTRITION
Calories 455; Sugars 0 g; Protein 32 g; Carbohydrate 39 g; Fat 20 g; Saturates 9 g

⭐⭐ easy

🕐 2 hrs 15 mins

🕐 20 mins

🍴 **COOK'S TIP**

If turbot is unavailable, then use halibut instead.

Marinated scallops are
chargrilled and served
with couscous studded
with colourful vegetables
and fresh herbs.

Chargrilled Scallops

SERVES 4

16 king scallops
3 tbsp olive oil
grated rind 1 lime
2 tbsp chopped fresh basil
2 tbsp snipped fresh chives
1 garlic clove, chopped finely
pepper

jewelled couscous

225 g/8 oz couscous
½ red pepper, deseeded and halved
½ yellow pepper, deseeded and halved
4 tbsp extra virgin olive oil
115 g/4 oz cucumber, chopped into
    1-cm/½-inch pieces
3 spring onions, chopped finely
1 tbsp lime juice
2 tbsp shredded fresh basil
salt and pepper

to garnish

fresh basil leaves
lime wedges

NUTRITION

Calories *401*; Sugars *3 g*; Protein *20 g*;
Carbohydrate *34 g*; Fat *21 g*; Saturates *3 g*

 moderate

2 hrs 15 mins

15 mins

1 Clean and trim the scallops as necessary, then put into a large, non-metallic dish. Mix the olive oil, lime rind, basil, chives, garlic and pepper together in a bowl, then pour over the scallops. Cover and leave to marinate in the refrigerator for 2 hours.

2 Cook the couscous according to the packet instructions, omitting any butter recommended. Brush the red and yellow pepper halves with a little of the olive oil and cook under a preheated hot grill for 8–10 minutes, turning once, until the skins are charred and blistered and the flesh is tender. Put into a polythene bag and leave until cool enough to handle. When cool, peel off the skins and chop the flesh into 1-cm/½-inch pieces. Add to the couscous with the remaining olive oil, cucumber, spring onions, lime juice and salt and pepper to taste. Reserve.

3 Lift the scallops from the marinade and thread on to 4 metal skewers. Transfer to a lit barbecue or preheated ridged griddle pan and cook for 1 minute on each side, until charred and firm, but not quite cooked through. Remove from the heat and leave to rest for 2 minutes.

4 Stir the shredded basil into the couscous and transfer to 4 serving plates. Put a skewer on each, garnish with basil leaves and lime wedges and serve.

These crisp little vegetable and prawn cakes make an ideal light lunch or supper, accompanied with a salad.

Prawn Röstis

1 To make the salsa, mix the tomatoes, mango, chilli, red onion, coriander, chives, olive oil, lemon juice and seasoning together. Leave to stand to allow the flavours to infuse.

2 Using a food processor or the fine blade of a box grater, finely grate the potatoes, celeriac, carrot and onion. Mix with the prawns, flour and egg. Season well with salt and pepper and reserve.

3 Divide the prawn mixture into 8 equal portions. Press each into a greased 10-cm/4-inch cutter (if you only have 1 cutter, simply shape the röstis individually).

4 Heat a shallow layer of vegetable oil in a large frying pan over a medium heat. When hot, transfer the vegetable and prawn cakes, still in the cutters, to the frying pan, in batches if necessary. When the oil sizzles underneath, remove the cutter. Fry gently, pressing down with a spatula, for 6–8 minutes on each side until crisp and browned and the vegetables are tender. Drain on kitchen paper. Serve immediately, while still hot, with the tomato salsa and mixed salad leaves.

 COOK'S TIP

The prawns can be replaced with small flakes of fresh cod, salmon or tuna if you prefer.

SERVES 4

350 g/12 oz potatoes
350 g/12 oz celeriac
1 carrot
½ small onion
225 g/8 oz cooked peeled prawns, thawed if frozen and well drained on kitchen paper
25 g/1 oz plain flour
1 egg, beaten lightly
50 ml/2 fl oz vegetable oil, for frying
salt and pepper
mixed salad leaves, to serve

cherry tomato salsa
225 g/8 oz mixed cherry tomatoes such as baby plum, yellow, orange, quartered
½ small mango, diced finely
1 red chilli, deseeded and finely chopped
½ small red onion, chopped finely
1 tbsp chopped fresh coriander
1 tbsp snipped fresh chives
2 tbsp olive oil
2 tsp lemon juice

NUTRITION
Calories *445*; Sugars *9 g*; Protein *19 g*; Carbohydrate *29 g*; Fat *29 g*; Saturates *4 g*

★★★   moderate
    20 mins
    12–16 mins

This dish is much revered in both Belgium and France. Try the chips with a little home-made mayonnaise (see Cod and Chips page 96) and enjoy a truly Belgian feast.

Moules Marinières

SERVES 4

900 g/2 lb live mussels
2 shallots, chopped finely
2 garlic cloves, chopped finely
150 ml/5 fl oz dry white wine
2 tbsp chopped fresh parsley
salt and pepper

chips
900 g/2 lb potatoes, peeled
600 ml/1 pint vegetable oil, for deep-frying
salt

to serve (optional)
lemon wedges
Mayonnaise (see page 96)

1 Clean the mussels by scrubbing or scraping the shells and pulling out any 'beards' that are attached to them. Discard any mussels with broken shells or any that refuse to close when tapped.

2 To make the chips, cut the potatoes into thin strips, about 1-cm/½-inch thick. Fill a large saucepan or chip pan about one-third full with vegetable oil and heat to 140°C/275°F, or until a cube of bread browns in 1 minute. Add the chips in 3 batches and cook for 5–6 minutes until the chips are tender, but not browned. Drain on kitchen paper.

3 Put the mussels into a large saucepan with the shallots, garlic and white wine. Cook, covered, over a high heat for 3–4 minutes until the mussels have opened. Discard any mussels that remain closed. Add the parsley and season to taste with salt and pepper, if necessary. Keep warm.

4 Increase the temperature of the oil to 190°C/375°F, or until a cube of bread browns in 30 seconds. Cook the chips, again in 3 batches, for 2–3 minutes until golden and crisp. Drain on kitchen paper and sprinkle with salt.

5 Transfer the mussels to 4 large serving bowls, then divide the chips between smaller bowls or plates and serve with lemon wedges and plenty of mayonnaise for dipping chips, if wished.

NUTRITION
Calories *88*; Sugars *1 g*; Protein *9 g*;
Carbohydrate *4 g*; Fat *14 g*; Saturates *0.5 g*

easy

15 mins

30 mins

This recipe conjures up southern France – tomatoes, wine, herbs and garlic combine to make a flavourful mussel stew.

Provençal Mussels

1 Clean the mussels by scrubbing or scraping the shells and pulling out any 'beards' that are attached to them. Discard any mussels with broken shells or any that do not close when tapped. Put the mussels into a large saucepan with just the water that clings to their shells. Cook, covered, over a high heat for 3–4 minutes until the mussels have opened. Discard any mussels that remain closed. Strain, reserving the cooking liquid. Reserve.

2 Heat the olive oil in a large saucepan over a low heat. Add the onion and cook gently for 8–10 minutes until softened, but not coloured. Add the garlic and thyme and cook for a further 1 minute. Add the red wine and simmer rapidly until reduced and syrupy. Add the tomatoes and strained, reserved mussel cooking liquid and bring to the boil. Cover and simmer for 30 minutes. Uncover and cook for a further 15 minutes.

3 Add the mussels and cook for a further 5 minutes until heated through. Stir in the parsley, season to taste with salt and pepper and serve.

SERVES 4

900 g/2 lb live mussels
3 tbsp olive oil
1 onion, chopped finely
3 garlic cloves, chopped finely
2 tsp fresh thyme leaves
150 ml/5 fl oz red wine
800 g/1 lb 12 oz canned chopped tomatoes
2 tbsp chopped fresh parsley
salt and pepper

 COOK'S TIP

Replace the mussels with an equal quantity of clams.

NUTRITION
Calories *194*; Sugars *5 g*; Protein *12 g*;
Carbohydrate *9 g*; Fat *10 g*; Saturates *2 g*

 moderate

10 mins

1 hr

Pasta, Potatoes *and* Grains

Nutritionists today recommend a diet high in complex carbohydrates, which include pasta, rice, potatoes, breads and grains. A diet based around this food group ensures high energy levels without any dips in blood sugar levels, which can lead to bingeing.

This chapter includes a variety of dishes based on these foods. The most popular of these has to be pasta and there are a number of pasta dishes here. There are also a variety of skill levels catered for, from very simple pasta dishes, like Spaghettini with Crab, and Linguini with Sardines, to more complicated dishes, like home-made Crab Ravioli, Fideua, and Seafood Lasagne.

There are also recipes for pies and pasties, such as Herring & Potato Pie, and Fish Pasties, as well as rice dishes, including Jambalaya, Lobster Risotto, and Prawn & Asparagus Risotto.

This is based on a Sicilian dish combining broccoli and anchovies, but in this recipe lemon and garlic have been added for more flavour.

Tagliatelle *with* Broccoli *and* Anchovies

SERVES 4

6 tbsp olive oil
50 g/1¾ oz fresh white breadcrumbs
450 g/1 lb broccoli, cut into small florets
350 g/12 oz dried tagliatelle
4 canned anchovy fillets,
  drained and chopped
2 garlic cloves, sliced
grated rind of 1 lemon
large pinch of crushed chillies
salt and pepper
freshly grated Parmesan cheese, to serve

1 Heat 2 tablespoons of the olive oil in a frying pan over a medium heat. Add the breadcrumbs and stir-fry for 4–5 minutes until golden and crisp. Drain on kitchen paper.

2 Bring a large saucepan of lightly salted water to the boil over a medium heat Add the broccoli and blanch for 3 minutes then drain, reserving the water. Refresh the broccoli under cold running water and drain again. Pat dry on kitchen paper and reserve. Bring the water back to the boil and add the tagliatelle. Cook according to the packet instructions until tender, but still firm to the bite.

3 Meanwhile, heat 2 tablespoons of the olive oil in a frying pan over a medium heat. Add the anchovies and cook for 1 minute, then mash with a wooden spoon to a paste. Add the garlic, lemon rind and crushed chillies and cook for 2 minutes. Add the broccoli and cook for a further 3–4 minutes until hot.

4 Drain the pasta and add to the broccoli with the remaining 2 tablespoons of olive oil. Season to taste with salt and pepper. Toss together. Divide the tagliatelle between 4 serving plates and top with the breadcrumbs and Parmesan cheese. Serve immediately.

NUTRITION
Calories 529; Sugars 4 g; Protein 17 g;
Carbohydrate 75 g; Fat 20 g; Saturates 3 g

easy

10 mins

30 mins

The story goes that this was a sauce made and eaten by Italian women, who needed a quick and simple meal to keep them going. Most of the ingredients you will have in the storecupboard.

Pasta Puttanesca

1 Heat the olive oil in a saucepan over a low heat. Add the onion, anchovies and crushed chillies. Cook for 10 minutes until softened and beginning to brown. Add the garlic and cook for 30 seconds.

2 Add the tomatoes and tomato purée and bring to the boil. Simmer gently for 10 minutes.

3 Meanwhile, bring a large saucepan of lightly salted water to the boil over a medium heat. Add the dried spaghetti and cook according to the packet instructions until tender, but still firm to the bite.

4 Add the olives, capers and sun-dried tomatoes to the sauce. Simmer for a further 2–3 minutes. Season to taste with salt and pepper.

5 Drain the pasta well and stir in the sauce. Toss well. Transfer to 4 large serving plates, garnish with tomato wedges and mixed fresh herbs and serve immediately.

SERVES 4

3 tbsp extra virgin olive oil
1 large red onion, chopped finely
4 canned anchovy fillets, drained
pinch of crushed chillies
2 garlic cloves, chopped finely
400 g/14 oz canned chopped tomatoes
2 tbsp tomato purée
225 g/8 oz dried spaghetti
25 g/1 oz stoned black olives,
   chopped roughly
25 g/1 oz stoned green olives,
   chopped roughly
1 tbsp capers, drained and rinsed
4 sun-dried tomatoes, chopped roughly
salt and pepper
mixed fresh herbs, to garnish

to garnish
mixed fresh herbs
tomato wedges

NUTRITION
Calories *359*; Sugars *10 g*; Protein *10 g*;
Carbohydrate *51 g*; Fat *14 g*; Saturates *2 g*

easy

5 mins

25 mins

🧑‍🍳 **COOK'S TIP**

Crushed chillies are available from large supermarkets, but if you cannot find them, then use a fresh red chilli, deseeded and sliced, instead.

A rich dish of layers of pasta, with seafood and mushrooms in a tomato sauce, topped with béchamel sauce and baked until golden.

Seafood Lasagne

SERVES 4

50 g/1¾ oz butter
40 g/1½ oz plain flour
1 tsp mustard powder
600 ml/1 pint milk
2 tbsp olive oil, plus extra for oiling
1 onion, chopped
2 garlic cloves, chopped finely
1 tbsp fresh thyme leaves
450 g/1 lb mixed mushrooms, sliced
150 ml/5 fl oz white wine
400 g/14 oz canned chopped tomatoes
450 g/1 lb mixed skinless white
   fish fillets, cubed
225 g/8 oz scallops, trimmed
4–6 sheets fresh lasagne
225 g/8 oz mozzarella cheese, chopped
salt and pepper

NUTRITION
Calories 790; Sugars 23 g; Protein 55 g;
Carbohydrate 74 g; Fat 32 g; Saturates 19 g

 moderate

 30 mins

1 hr 20 mins

1 Melt the butter in a saucepan over a low heat. Add the flour and mustard powder and stir until smooth. Simmer gently for 2 minutes without colouring. Gradually add the milk, whisking until smooth. Bring to the boil and simmer for 2 minutes. Remove from the heat and reserve. Cover the surface of the sauce with clingfilm to prevent a skin forming.

2 Heat the olive oil in a large frying pan over a low heat. Add the onion, garlic and thyme and cook gently for 5 minutes until softened. Add the mushrooms and fry for a further 5 minutes until softened. Stir in the wine and boil rapidly until nearly evaporated. Stir in the tomatoes. Bring to the boil and simmer, covered, for 15 minutes. Season to taste with salt and pepper and reserve.

3 Lightly oil a lasagne dish with a little olive oil. Spoon half the tomato sauce over the base of the dish and top with half the fish and scallops.

4 Layer half the lasagne over the fish, pour over half the white sauce and add half the mozzarella cheese. Repeat these layers, finishing with the white sauce and mozzarella cheese.

5 Bake in a preheated oven, 200°C/400°F/Gas Mark 6, for 35–40 minutes until bubbling and golden and the fish is cooked through. Remove from the oven and leave to stand on a heat resistant surface for 10 minutes before serving.

This is a very full-flavoured and elegant-looking dish, especially if you can find small clams, which often have richly coloured shells.

Spaghetti *al* Vongole

1 Put the clams into a large saucepan with just the water clinging to their shells and cook, covered, over a high heat for 3–4 minutes, shaking the pan occasionally, until the clams have opened. Remove from the heat and strain, reserving the cooking liquid. Discard any clams that remain closed. Reserve.

2 Heat the olive oil in a saucepan over a low heat. Add the onion and cook for 10 minutes until softened, but not coloured. Add the garlic and thyme and cook for 30 seconds. Increase the heat and add the white wine. Simmer rapidly until reduced and syrupy. Add the tomatoes and reserved clam cooking liquid. Cover and simmer for 15 minutes. Uncover and simmer for a further 15 minutes until thickened. Season to taste with salt and pepper.

3 Meanwhile, bring a large saucepan of lightly salted water to the boil over a medium heat. Add the spaghetti and cook until tender, but still firm to the bite. Drain and return to the pan.

4 Add the clams to the tomato sauce and heat through for 2–3 minutes. Add the parsley and stir well. Add the tomato sauce to the pasta and toss together until the pasta is well coated in sauce. Transfer to a large serving dish and garnish with thyme. Serve.

SERVES 4

900 g/2 lb live clams, scrubbed
2 tbsp olive oil
1 large onion, chopped finely
2 garlic cloves, chopped finely
1 tsp fresh thyme leaves
150 ml/5 fl oz white wine
400 g/14 oz canned chopped tomatoes
350 g/12 oz dried spaghetti
1 tbsp chopped fresh parsley
salt and pepper
fresh thyme leaves, to garnish

NUTRITION

Calories 471; Sugars 9 g; Protein 24 g; Carbohydrate 75 g; Fat 8 g; Saturates 1 g

easy

10 mins

1 hr

(🧑‍🍳) COOK'S TIP

If you are only able to get very large clams, reserve a few in their shells to garnish and shell the rest.

This is a very quick dish that is ideal for mid-week suppers as it is so simple to prepare, but full of flavour.

Linguini *with* Sardines

SERVES 4

8 sardines, filleted
1 fennel bulb
4 tbsp olive oil
3 garlic cloves, sliced
1 tsp crushed chillies
350 g/12 oz dried linguine
½ tsp finely grated lemon rind
1 tbsp lemon juice
2 tbsp pine kernels, toasted
2 tbsp chopped fresh parsley,
    plus extra for sprinkling
salt and pepper
fresh herbs, to garnish

1 Wash the sardine fillets under cold running water and pat dry with kitchen paper. Roughly chop into large pieces and reserve. Trim the fennel bulb and slice very thinly.

2 Heat 2 tablespoons of the olive oil in a large frying pan over a medium heat. Add the garlic and crushed chillies and cook for 1 minute, then add the fennel. Cook over a medium–high heat for 4–5 minutes until softened. Add the sardine pieces and cook for a further 3–4 minutes until just cooked.

3 Meanwhile, bring a large saucepan of lightly salted water to the boil over a medium heat. Add the linguini and cook until tender, but still firm to the bite. Drain well and return to the pan.

4 Add the lemon rind, lemon juice, pine kernels, parsley and seasoning to the sardines and toss together. Add to the pasta with the remaining olive oil and toss together gently. Transfer the pasta to 4 large serving bowls, sprinkle with parsley and garnish with fresh herbs. Serve immediately.

NUTRITION
Calories 547; Sugars 5 g; Protein 23 g;
Carbohydrate 68 g; Fat 23 g; Saturates 3 g

 easy

 10 mins

🕐 12 mins

🍲 **COOK'S TIP**

Reserve 2 tablespoons of the pasta cooking water and add to the pasta with the sauce if the mixture seems a little dry.

The classic Italian combination of pasta and tuna is enhanced in this recipe with a delicious parsley sauce.

Spaghetti *al* Tonno

1 Drain the tuna thoroughly. Put the tuna into a food processor or blender, together with the anchovies, olive oil and the parsley and process until the sauce is very smooth.

2 Spoon the crème fraîche into the food processor or blender and process again for a few seconds to blend. Season to taste with salt and pepper.

3 Bring a large saucepan of lightly salted water to the boil over a medium heat. Add the spaghetti and cook according to the packet instructions until tender, but still firm to the bite.

4 Drain the spaghetti, return to the pan and place over a medium heat. Add the butter and toss well to coat. Spoon in the sauce and quickly toss into the spaghetti, using 2 forks.

5 Remove the pan from the heat and transfer the spaghetti to 4 warmed serving plates. Garnish with the olives and a few sprigs of fresh parsley and serve immediately.

SERVES 4

200 g/7 oz canned tuna
60 g/2 oz canned anchovy fillets, drained
225 ml/8 fl oz olive oil
55 g/2 oz roughly chopped
    flat-leaved parsley
150 ml/5 fl oz crème fraîche
450 g/1 lb dried spaghetti
25 g/1 oz butter
salt and pepper

to garnish
stoned black olives
fresh flat-leaved parsley sprigs

NUTRITION
Calories *1065*; Sugars *3 g*; Protein *27 g*;
Carbohydrate *52 g*; Fat *85 g*; Saturates *18 g*

  easy

10 mins

15 mins

Fideua is a pasta dish from the area south of Valencia, in western Spain. It is very like a paella, but is made with very fine pasta instead of rice.

Fideua

SERVES 6

3 tbsp olive oil

1 large onion, chopped

2 garlic cloves, chopped finely

pinch of saffron threads, crushed

½ tsp paprika

3 tomatoes, peeled, deseeded and chopped

350 g/12 oz egg vermicelli, broken roughly into 5-cm/2-inch lengths

150 ml/5 fl oz white wine

300 ml/10 fl oz fish stock

12 large raw prawns

18 live mussels, scrubbed and bearded

350 g/12 oz cleaned squid, cut into rings

18 large, live clams, scrubbed

2 tbsp chopped fresh parsley

salt and pepper

1 Heat the olive oil in a large frying pan or paella pan over a low heat. Add the onion and cook gently for 5 minutes until softened. Add the garlic and cook for a further 30 seconds. Add the saffron and paprika and stir well. Add the tomatoes and cook for a further 2–3 minutes until they have collapsed.

2 Add the vermicelli and stir well. Add the white wine and boil rapidly until the wine has been absorbed.

3 Add the stock, prawns, mussels, squid and clams. Stir and return to a simmer for 10 minutes until the prawns and squid are cooked through and the mussels and clams have opened. The stock should be almost absorbed.

4 Add the parsley and season to taste with salt and pepper. Transfer to 6 large, warmed serving bowls and serve immediately.

NUTRITION

Calories 373; Sugars 4 g; Protein 23 g; Carbohydrate 52 g; Fat 8 g; Saturates 1 g

 ⭐⭐⭐ moderate

🕐 40 mins

🕐 20 mins

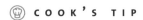 COOK'S TIP

Use whatever combination of seafood you prefer. Try langoustines, prawns, clams and monkfish.

The classic Thai noodle dish is flavoured with fish sauce, roasted peanuts and prawns.

Thai Noodles

1 Drain the prawns on kitchen paper to remove excess moisture. Reserve. Cook the rice noodles according to the packet instructions. Drain well and reserve.

2 Heat the vegetable oil in a preheated wok or large frying pan over a high heat. Add the garlic and fry until just golden. Add the egg and stir quickly to break it up. Cook for a few seconds.

3 Add the prawns and noodles, scraping down the sides of the wok to ensure they mix with the egg and garlic.

4 Add the lemon juice, Thai fish sauce, sugar, half the peanuts, cayenne, the spring onions and half the beansprouts, stirring quickly all the time. Cook over a high heat for a further 2 minutes until heated through.

5 Transfer to 4 serving plates, top with the remaining peanuts and beansprouts and sprinkle with the coriander. Garnish with lemon wedges and serve.

SERVES 4

350 g/12 oz cooked peeled tiger prawns
115 g/4 oz flat rice noodles or rice vermicelli
4 tbsp vegetable oil
2 garlic cloves, chopped finely
1 egg
2 tbsp lemon juice
1½ tbsp Thai fish sauce
½ tsp sugar
2 tbsp chopped, roasted peanuts
½ tsp cayenne pepper
2 spring onions, cut into 2.5-cm/1-inch pieces
50 g/1¾ oz fresh beansprouts
1 tbsp chopped fresh coriander
lemon wedges, to garnish

NUTRITION
Calories *344*; Sugars *2 g*; Protein *21 g*;
Carbohydrate *27 g*; Fat *17 g*; Saturates *2 g*

easy

10 mins

5 mins

 COOK'S TIP

This is a basic dish to which lots of different cooked seafood could be added. Cooked squid rings, mussels and langoustines would all work well.

124

Originally, kedgeree or khichri was a Hindi dish of rice and lentils, varied with fish or meat in all kinds of ways. It has come to be a dish of rice, spices and smoked fish served with hard-boiled eggs, often for breakfast.

Kedgeree

SERVES 4

450 g/1 lb undyed smoked haddock fillet
2 tbsp olive oil
1 large onion, chopped
2 garlic cloves, chopped finely
½ tsp ground turmeric
½ tsp ground cumin
1 tsp ground coriander
175 g/6 oz basmati rice
4 medium eggs
25 g/1 oz butter
1 tbsp chopped fresh parsley

NUTRITION
Calories 457; Sugars 3 g; Protein 33 g;
Carbohydrate 40 g; Fat 18 g; Saturates 6 g

easy

15 mins

35 mins

1 Put the haddock fillet in a large, shallow dish and pour over enough boiling water to cover. Leave to stand for 10 minutes. Lift the fish from the cooking water, discard the skin and bones and flake the fish. Reserve both the fish and the cooking water.

2 Heat the olive oil in a large saucepan over a medium heat. Add the onion and cook for 10 minutes until beginning to brown. Add the garlic and cook for a further 30 seconds. Add the turmeric, cumin and coriander and stir-fry for 30 seconds until the spices smell fragrant. Add the rice and stir well.

3 Measure 350 ml/12 fl oz of the reserved cooking water and add to the pan. Stir well and bring to the boil. Cover and cook over a very low heat for 12–15 minutes until the rice is tender and the stock is absorbed.

4 Meanwhile, bring a saucepan of water to the boil over a medium heat. Add the eggs, return to the boil and cook for 8 minutes. Immediately drain the eggs and refresh under cold running water to stop them cooking. Reserve.

5 Add the reserved fish pieces, the butter and parsley to the rice. Turn into a large serving dish. Shell and quarter the eggs and arrange on top of the rice. Serve immediately.

This is a modern version of the classic dish, using smoked salmon as well as fresh salmon and lots of herbs. This is suitable for a smart dinner party and would serve six as a starter or four as a main course.

Modern Kedgeree

1 Melt the butter with the olive oil in a large saucepan over a low heat. Add the onion and cook gently for 10 minutes until softened, but not coloured. Add the garlic and cook for a further 30 seconds.

2 Add the rice and cook for 2–3 minutes, stirring constantly, until transparent. Add the fish stock and stir well. Bring to the boil, cover and simmer very gently for 10 minutes.

3 Remove the pan from the heat and add the salmon fillet and the smoked salmon. Stir well, adding a little more stock or water if it seems dry. Return to the heat and cook for a further 6–8 minutes until the fish and rice are tender and all the stock is absorbed.

4 Remove the pan from the heat and stir in the cream, dill and spring onions. Season to taste with salt and pepper and transfer to a large serving dish. Garnish with lemon slices and a few sprigs of fresh dill and serve.

SERVES 4

25 g/1 oz butter
1 tbsp olive oil
1 onion, chopped finely
1 garlic clove, chopped finely
175 g g/6 oz long-grain rice
400 ml/14 fl oz fish stock
175 g/6 oz skinless, boneless salmon fillet, chopped
85 g/3 oz smoked salmon, chopped
2 tbsp double cream
2 tbsp chopped fresh dill
3 spring onions, chopped finely
salt and pepper

to garnish
lemon slices
fresh dill sprigs

NUTRITION
Calories 370; Sugars 3 g; Protein 10 g; Carbohydrate 39 g; Fat 19 g; Saturates 9 g

 easy

 10 mins

35 mins

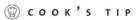 **COOK'S TIP**

Use smoked salmon trimmings for a budget dish.

Jambalaya is a dish of Cajun origin. There are as many versions of this dish as there are people who cook it. Here is a straightforward one, using prawns, chicken and smoked sausage.

Jambalaya

SERVES 4

2 tbsp vegetable oil
2 onions, chopped roughly
1 green pepper, deseeded and
   roughly chopped
2 celery sticks, chopped roughly
3 garlic cloves, chopped finely
2 tsp paprika
300 g/10½ oz skinless, boneless chicken
   breasts, chopped
100 g/3½ oz kabanos sausages, chopped
3 tomatoes, peeled and chopped
450 g/1 lb long-grain rice
850 ml/1½ pints hot chicken or fish stock
1 tsp dried oregano
2 bay leaves
12 large raw prawn tails
4 spring onions, chopped finely
2 tbsp chopped fresh parsley
salt and pepper
fresh herbs, to garnish

NUTRITION
Calories *283*; Sugars *3 g*; Protein *33 g*;
Carbohydrate *40 g*; Fat *18 g*; Saturates *6 g*

 easy

 15 mins

   35 mins

1 Heat the vegetable oil in a large frying pan over a low heat. Add the onions, pepper, celery and garlic and cook for 8–10 minutes until all the vegetables have softened. Add the paprika and cook for a further 30 seconds. Add the chicken and sausages and cook for 8–10 minutes until lightly browned. Add the tomatoes and cook for 2–3 minutes until they have collapsed.

2 Add the rice to the pan and stir well. Pour in the hot stock, oregano and bay leaves and stir well. Cover and simmer for 10 minutes.

3 Add the prawns and stir. Cover again and cook for a further 6–8 minutes until the rice is tender and the prawns are cooked through.

4 Stir in the spring onions and parsley and season to taste with salt and pepper. Transfer to a large serving dish, garnish with fresh herbs and serve.

COOK'S TIP

Jambalaya is a dish, which has a few basic ingredients – onions, green peppers, celery, rice and seasonings – to which you can add whatever you have to hand.

This is a special occasion dish, just for two. You could easily double the recipe for a dinner party.

Lobster Risotto

1 To prepare the lobster, remove the claws by twisting. Crack the claws using the back of a large knife and reserve. Split the body lengthways. Remove and discard the intestinal vein, which runs down the tail, the stomach sac and the spongy looking gills. Remove the meat from the tail and roughly chop. Reserve with the claws.

2 Heat half the butter and olive oil in a large frying pan over a low heat. Add the onion and cook for 4–5 minutes until softened. Add the garlic and cook for a further 30 seconds. Add the thyme and rice. Stir well for 1–2 minutes, until the rice is coated in the butter and oil and begins to look translucent.

3 Keep the stock on a low heat. Increase the heat under the frying pan to medium and begin adding the stock, a ladleful at a time, stirring well between each addition. Continue until all the stock has been absorbed. This should take 20–25 minutes.

4 Add the reserved lobster meat and claws. Stir in the wine, increasing the heat. When the wine is absorbed, remove from the heat and stir in the peppercorns, the remaining butter and parsley. Leave to stand for 1 minute, then transfer to 2 serving plates. Garnish with lemon and dill and serve.

SERVES 2

1 cooked lobster, about 400–450 g/14 oz–1 lb
50 g/1¾ oz butter
1 tbsp olive oil
1 onion, chopped finely
1 garlic clove, chopped finely
1 tsp fresh thyme leaves
175 g/6 oz arborio rice
600 ml/1 pint hot fish stock
150 ml/5 fl oz sparkling wine
1 tsp green or pink peppercorns in brine, drained and roughly chopped
1 tbsp chopped fresh parsley

to garnish
lemon slices
fresh dill sprigs

 COOK'S TIP

For a slightly cheaper version substitute 450 g/1 lb prawns for the lobster.

NUTRITION
Calories *487*; Sugars *8 g*; Protein *10 g*;
Carbohydrate *86 g*; Fat *10 g*; Saturates *2 g*

 ★★★   moderate

15 mins

35 mins

This unusual and striking
dish with fresh prawns and
asparagus is very simple
to prepare and ideal for
impromptu supper parties.

Prawn *and* Asparagus Risotto

SERVES 4

1.2 litres/2 pints vegetable stock
375 g/13 oz asparagus, cut into
   5-cm/2-inch lengths
2 tbsp olive oil
1 onion, chopped finely
1 garlic clove, chopped finely
350 g/12 oz arborio rice
450 g/1 lb raw tiger prawns, peeled
   and deveined
2 tbsp olive paste or tapenade
2 tbsp chopped fresh basil
salt and pepper

to garnish
fresh Parmesan cheese shavings
cooked whole prawns, unpeeled
fresh dill sprigs

1 Put the stock into a saucepan and bring to the boil over a low heat. Add the asparagus and cook for 3 minutes until tender. Strain, reserving the stock, and refresh the asparagus under cold running water. Drain and reserve.

2 Heat the olive oil in a large frying pan over a low heat. Add the onion and cook gently for 5 minutes until softened. Add the garlic and cook for a further 30 seconds. Add the rice and stir for 1–2 minutes until coated with the oil and slightly translucent.

3 Keep the stock on a low heat. Increase the heat under the frying pan to medium and begin adding the stock, a ladleful at a time, stirring well after each addition. Continue until almost all the stock has been absorbed. This should take 20–25 minutes.

4 Add the prawns and asparagus with the last ladleful of stock and cook for a further 5 minutes until the prawns and rice are tender and the stock has been absorbed. Remove the pan from the heat.

5 Stir in the olive paste, basil and salt and pepper to taste and leave to stand for 1 minute. Transfer to 4 serving bowls and garnish with Parmesan cheese shavings, whole prawns and a few sprigs of fresh dill. Serve immediately.

NUTRITION
Calories *566*; Sugars *4 g*; Protein *30 g*;
Carbohydrate *86 g*; Fat *14 g*; Saturates *2 g*

   moderate
   10 mins
   40 mins

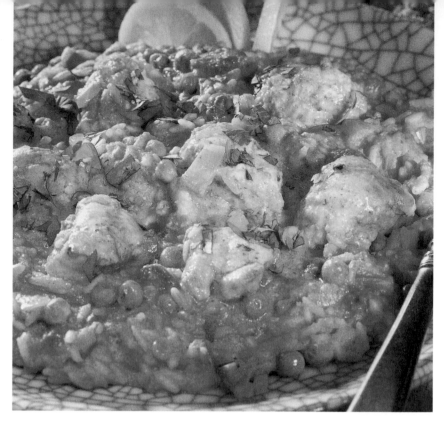

A Thai-influenced dish of rice cooked in coconut milk, with spicy-cooked monkfish and fresh peas.

Spicy Coconut Rice *with* Monkfish

1 Put both chillies, garlic, saffron, mint, olive oil and lemon juice into a food processor or blender and process until finely chopped, but not smooth.

2 Put the monkfish into a large, non-metallic dish and pour over the spice paste, mixing together well. Cover and leave to marinate in the refrigerator for 20 minutes.

3 Heat a large saucepan until very hot over a medium heat. Using a slotted spoon, lift the monkfish from the marinade and add in batches to the hot pan. Cook for 3–4 minutes until browned and firm. Remove with a slotted spoon and reserve.

4 Add the onion and remaining marinade to the same pan and cook for about 5 minutes until softened and lightly browned. Add the rice and stir until well coated. Add the tomatoes and coconut milk. Bring to the boil, cover and simmer very gently for 15 minutes. Stir in the peas, season to taste with salt and pepper and arrange the fish over the top. Cover with foil and continue to cook over a very low heat for 5 minutes. Transfer to 4 large serving plates and garnish with lemon slices and chopped coriander. Serve immediately.

SERVES 4

1 fresh red chilli, deseeded and chopped
1 tsp crushed chillies
2 garlic cloves, chopped
2 pinches of saffron threads
3 tbsp chopped roughly mint leaves
4 tbsp olive oil
2 tbsp lemon juice
375 g/12 oz monkfish fillet, cut into bite-sized pieces
1 onion, chopped finely
225 g/8 oz long-grain rice
400g/14 oz canned chopped tomatoes
200 ml/7 fl oz coconut milk
115 g/4 oz fresh peas
salt and pepper

to garnish
lemon slices
2 tbsp chopped fresh coriander

NUTRITION

Calories *440*; Sugars *8 g*; Protein *22 g*; Carbohydrate *60 g*; Fat *14 g*; Saturates *2 g*

easy

30 mins

30 mins

COOK'S TIP

When marinating fish, make sure the fish is placed in a large, shallow, non-metallic dish and covered with clingfilm.

Based on a traditional Cuban recipe, this dish is similar to Spanish paella, but it has the added kick of dark rum. Choose any firm white fish, such as cod or monkfish.

Fish *and* Rice *with* Dark Rum

SERVES 4

450 g/1 lb firm white fish fillets, skinned and cut into 2.5-cm/1-inch cubes
2 tsp ground cumin
2 tsp dried oregano
2 tbsp lime juice
150 ml/5 fl oz dark rum
1 tbsp dark muscovado sugar
3 garlic cloves, chopped finely
1 large onion, chopped
1 medium red pepper, deseeded and sliced into rings
1 medium green pepper, deseeded and sliced into rings
1 medium yellow pepper, deseeded and sliced into rings
1.2 litres/2 pints fish stock
350 g/12 oz long-grain rice
salt and pepper
crusty bread, to serve

to garnish
fresh oregano leaves
lime wedges

NUTRITION
Calories *547*; Sugars *9 g*; Protein *27 g*; Carbohydrate *85 g*; Fat *4 g*; Saturates *1 g*

moderate

2 hrs 35 mins

35 mins

1 Place the cubes of fish in a bowl and add the cumin, oregano, lime juice, rum and sugar. Season to taste with salt and pepper. Mix thoroughly, cover with clingfilm and leave to chill in the refrigerator for 2 hours.

2 Meanwhile, place the garlic, onion and peppers in a large saucepan. Pour in the stock and stir in the rice. Bring to the boil over a medium heat, then reduce the heat cover and simmer for 15 minutes.

3 Gently stir in the fish and the marinade juices. Bring back to the boil and simmer, uncovered, stirring occasionally, but taking care not to break up the fish, for about 10 minutes until the fish is cooked through and the rice is tender.

4 Season to taste with salt and pepper and transfer to a warmed serving plate. Garnish with fresh oregano and lime wedges and serve with crusty bread.

COOK'S TIP

When buying dried spices and herbs, buy in small quantities and store in a cool dark place in order to preserve their flavour and aroma.

This is a rich French stew of fish and vegetables, flavoured with saffron and herbs. Traditionally, the fish and vegetables, and the soup, are served separately.

Cotriade

1 Using a mortar and pestle, crush the saffron and add to the fish stock. Stir and leave to infuse for at least 10 minutes.

2 Heat the olive oil and butter together in a large saucepan over a low heat. Add the onion and cook gently for 4–5 minutes until softened. Add the garlic, leek, fennel and potatoes. Cover and cook for a further 10–15 minutes until the vegetables are softened.

3 Add the wine and simmer rapidly for 3–4 minutes until reduced by half. Add the thyme, bay leaves and tomatoes and stir well. Add the saffron-infused fish stock. Bring to the boil, cover and simmer gently for 15 minutes until the vegetables are tender.

4 Add the fish, return to the boil and simmer for a further 3–4 minutes until all the fish is tender. Add the parsley and season to taste with salt and pepper. Using a slotted spoon, remove the fish and vegetables to a warmed serving dish and garnish with a few sprigs of fresh dill and lemon slices. Serve immediately.

SERVES 6

large pinch of saffron strands
600 ml/1 pint hot fish stock
1 tbsp olive oil
25 g/1 oz butter
1 onion, sliced
2 garlic cloves, chopped
1 leek, sliced
1 small fennel bulb, sliced finely
450 g/1 lb potatoes, cut into chunks
150 ml/5 fl oz dry white wine
1 tbsp fresh thyme leaves
2 bay leaves
4 ripe tomatoes, peeled and chopped
900 g/2 lb mixed fish such as haddock, hake, mackerel, red or grey mullet, chopped roughly
2 tbsp chopped fresh parsley
salt and pepper

to garnish
fresh dill sprigs
lemon slices

NUTRITION
Calories *81*; Sugars *0.9 g*; Protein *7.4 g*; Carbohydrate *3.8 g*; Fat *3.9 g*; Saturates *1.1 g*

 moderate

15 mins

 40 mins

 COOK'S TIP

Once the fish and vegetables have been cooked, the soup could be liquidised and rubbed through a sieve to give a smooth fish soup.

Traditionally, a pizza topped with mixed seafood would have no cheese, but in this case it helps to protect the fish from overcooking as well as adding texture.

Pizza Marinara

SERVES 4

225 g/8 oz strong white bread flour, plus extra for dusting
1 tsp salt
1 sachet easy-blend yeast
2 tbsp olive oil, plus extra for oiling
150 ml/5 fl oz hand-hot water

tomato sauce

2 tbsp olive oil
1 small onion, chopped finely
1 garlic clove, crushed
400 g/14 oz canned chopped tomatoes
1 tsp dried oregano
1 tbsp tomato purèe
salt and pepper

mixed seafood

16 live mussels, scrubbed and bearded
16 large, live clams, scrubbed
1 tbsp olive oil
12 raw tiger prawns
225 g/8 oz cleaned squid, cut into rings
350 g/112 oz mozzarella cheese, sliced
olive oil, for drizzling
handful of fresh basil leaves

NUTRITION

Calories *638*; Sugars *5 g*; Protein *55 g*;
Carbohydrate *50 g*; Fat *26 g*; Saturates *11 g*

 moderate

 1 hr 15 mins

25 mins

1 To make the pizza base, mix the flour, salt and yeast together in a bowl. Add the olive oil and enough water to form a firm dough. Knead the dough on a floured work surface until smooth and elastic. Form the dough into a ball and drop into an oiled bowl. Lightly oil the top of the dough, cover with a tea towel and leave to rise in a warm place for 1 hour or until doubled in bulk.

2 Meanwhile, make the sauce. Heat the olive oil in a saucepan over a medium heat. Add the onion and cook for 5 minutes until softened. Add the garlic and cook for a few seconds. Add the tomatoes, oregano, tomato purée and seasoning. Bring to the boil and simmer for 30 minutes. Leave to cool.

3 Put the mussels and clams into a pan with only the water that clings to their shells. Cover and cook over a high heat for 3–4 minutes until the shells have opened. Discard any that remain closed. Strain and discard the cooking liquid. Remove the seafood from their shells and reserve.

4 Heat the olive oil in a frying pan over a medium heat. Add the prawns and squid and cook until the prawns have turned pink and the squid is firm.

5 Put 2 baking sheets into a preheated oven, 230°C/450°F/Gas Mark 8. Knock back the dough and divide into 2. Shape into 25-cm/10-inch rounds. Put on to floured baking sheets.

6 Spread half the sauce on each pizza and add the seafood. Season and top with the cheese. Drizzle with olive oil and sit the sheets on top of the preheated sheets. Cook for 12–15 minutes, sprinkle with basil and serve.

This is a variation of Pissaladière, the classic French tart of slow-cooked onions on a bread base, very like a pizza.

Onion *and* Tuna Tart

1 To make the topping, heat the butter and olive oil in a saucepan over a very low heat. Add the onions and stir well. Cover and cook for 20 minutes. Add the sugar and salt. Cook, covered for a further 30–40 minutes, stirring until collapsed and beginning to brown. Uncover and cook for 15–10 minutes until evenly golden. Remove from the heat, stir in the thyme and season to taste with salt and pepper.

2 Meanwhile, make the base. Mix the flour, salt and yeast together in a bowl. Add the olive oil and enough water to form a soft dough. Knead the dough on a lightly floured work surface for 5 minutes until smooth and elastic.

3 Form the dough into a neat ball and drop into a lightly oiled bowl. Lightly oil the top of the dough, cover with a clean tea towel and leave to rise in a warm place for about 1 hour, or until doubled in bulk.

4 Put a baking sheet into a preheated oven, 220°C/425°F/Gas Mark 7. Knock back the risen dough by punching down the centre with your fist. Tip on to the work surface and knead briefly. Roll out the dough to fit a lightly oiled Swiss roll tin measuring 33 x 23 cm/13 x 9 inches, leaving a rim. You may have to stretch the dough to fit the tin as it is very springy.

5 Spread the onions in an even layer over the dough. Flake the tuna and put on top of the onions. Arrange the olives over the tuna and season with pepper. Transfer the tin to the preheated baking sheet and cook for 20 minutes until the dough is golden. Serve immediately.

SERVES 4

225 g/8 oz strong white bread flour, plus extra for dusting
1 tsp salt
1 sachet easy-blend yeast
2 tbsp olive oil, plus extra for oiling
150 ml/5 fl oz hand-hot water

topping
50 g/1¾ oz butter
2 tbsp olive oil
900 g/2 lb onions, sliced finely
1 tsp sugar
1 tsp salt
1 tsp fresh thyme leaves
200 g/7 oz canned tuna, drained
85 g/3 oz stoned black olives
salt and pepper

NUTRITION
Calories *541*; Sugars *14 g*; Protein *22 g*; Carbohydrate *61 g*; Fat *25 g*; Saturates *9 g*

★★★   moderate

    30 mins

    2 hrs

This is a delicious seafood variation of a classic Cornish pasty. Choose any firm white fish such as cod and serve either hot or cold with a fresh, crisp salad.

Fish Pasties

SERVES 4

450 g/1 lb self-raising flour,
    plus extra for dusting
pinch of salt
225 g/8 oz butter, diced, plus extra for greasing
2–3 tbsp cold water
1 egg, beaten lightly

filling

50 g/1¾ oz butter
80 g/3 oz leek, diced
80 g/3 oz onion, chopped finely
80 g/3 oz carrot, diced
225 g/8 oz potato, peeled and diced
350 g/12 oz firm white fish, cut into
    2.5-cm/1-inch pieces
4 tsp white wine vinegar
25 g/1 oz Cheddar cheese, grated
1 tsp chopped fresh tarragon
salt and pepper

to serve

mixed salad leaves
cherry tomatoes, halved

NUTRITION

Calories *250*; Sugars *1.2 g*; Protein *7 g*;
Carbohydrate *23.5 g*; Fat *15 g*; Saturates *9.4 g*

⭐⭐⭐   moderate

🕐   40 mins

🕐   35 mins

1 Sift the flour and salt together into a large bowl. Add the butter and rub it in with your fingertips until the mixture resembles coarse breadcrumbs. Add enough cold water to form a dough. Knead briefly until smooth. Wrap in clingfilm and leave to chill in the refrigerator for 30 minutes.

2 To make the filling, melt half the butter in a large frying pan over a low heat. Add the leek, onion and carrot and cook gently for 7–8 minutes until the vegetables are softened. Remove from the heat and leave to cool slightly.

3 Put the vegetable mixture into a bowl and add the potato, fish, vinegar, remaining butter, cheese, tarragon and salt and pepper to taste. Reserve.

4 Remove the pastry from the refrigerator and roll out thinly. Using a pastry cutter, press out four 19-cm/7½-inch discs. Alternatively, use a small plate of a similar size. Divide the filling between the 4 discs. Moisten the edges of the pastry and fold over. Pinch to seal. Crimp the edges and place the pasties on a lightly greased baking sheet. Brush generously with the beaten egg, avoiding the base of the pastry to prevent the pasties sticking to it.

5 Bake in a preheated oven, 200°C/400°F/Gas Mark 6, for 15 minutes. Remove from the oven and brush again with the egg glaze. Return to the oven for a further 20 minutes. Serve with mixed salad leaves and tomatoes.

Buckwheat flour is traditionally used in Breton pancakes. It is available from large supermarkets and health food shops.

Buckwheat Pancakes *with* Smoked Salmon

1 For the filling, mix the crème fraîche, capers, spring onions, red chilli, dill, chives, lemon rind and salt and pepper together in a small bowl. Reserve.

2 To make the buckwheat pancakes, sift the flours and salt together into a large bowl. Make a well in the centre and add the eggs. Mix the milk and water together and add half this mixture to the flour and eggs. Mix until smooth. Gradually add the remaining milk until you have a smooth batter. Stir in the melted butter.

3 Heat a 20-cm/8-inch pancake pan or frying pan over a medium heat. Dip a piece of wadded kitchen paper into a little vegetable oil and rub this over the surface of the pan to give a thin coating. Ladle about 2 tablespoons of pancake mixture to the pan, tilting and shaking the pan to coat the base evenly. Cook for 1 minute until the edges begin to lift away from the pan. Using a large palette knife, carefully lift the pancake and turn it over. It should be pale golden brown. Cook for 30 seconds on the second side. Remove from the pan and place on a warmed plate. Re-grease and reheat the pan and repeat with the remaining mixture to make 12–14 pancakes, depending on their thickness.

4 Place a slice of smoked salmon on each pancake and top with 2 teaspoons of the crème fraîche mixture. Fold the pancake in half and then in half again to form a triangle. Transfer to 4 serving plates, garnish with lemon slices and a few sprigs of fresh dill and serve.

SERVES 4

55 g/2 oz plain flour
55 g/2 oz buckwheat flour
pinch of salt
2 large eggs
200 ml/7 fl oz milk
85 ml/3 fl oz water
25 g/1 oz butter, melted
50 ml/2 fl oz vegetable oil, for frying
lemon slices and dill sprigs, to garnish

filling

125 ml/4 fl oz crème fraîche
1 tbsp capers, drained, rinsed and
  roughly chopped
3 spring onions, chopped finely
1 fresh red chilli, deseeded and
  finely chopped
1 tbsp chopped fresh dill, plus fresh dill
  sprigs to garnish
1 tbsp snipped fresh chives
1 tsp lemon rind
225 g/8 oz sliced smoked salmon
salt and pepper

NUTRITION
Calories *385*; Sugars *4 g*; Protein *24 g*;
Carbohydrate *27 g*; Fat *21 g*; Saturates *9 g*

 moderate

25 mins

 25 mins

This is a typical Chinese breakfast dish, although it is probably best served as a lunch or supper dish at a Western table!

Crab Congee

SERVES 4

225 g/8 oz short-grain rice
1.5 litres/2½ pints fish stock
½ tsp salt
100 g/3½ oz Chinese sausage, sliced thinly
225 g/8 oz white crab meat
6 spring onions, sliced
2 tbsp chopped fresh coriander
pepper, to serve

1 Place the rice in a large preheated wok or frying pan.

2 Add the stock to the wok and bring to the boil over a medium heat.

3 Reduce the heat, then simmer for 1 hour, stirring the mixture occasionally.

4 Add the salt, sliced Chinese sausage, white crab meat, sliced spring onions and chopped coriander to the wok and heat through for about 5 minutes.

5 Add a little more water to the wok if the congee 'porridge' is too thick, stirring well.

6 Transfer the crab congee to 4 warmed serving bowls, sprinkle with freshly ground black pepper and serve immediately.

NUTRITION

Calories 327; Sugars 0.1 g; Protein 18 g;
Carbohydrate 50 g; Fat 7 g; Saturates 2 g

easy

5 mins

1 hr 15 mins

 **COOK'S TIP**

If using fresh crab, always choose crabs that are heavy for their size and ones that do not sound watery when shaken.

This combination of assorted seafood and tender vegetables flavoured with ginger makes an ideal light meal when served with freshly cooked egg thread noodles.

Seafood Stir-fry

1 Bring a small saucepan of water to the boil over a medium heat. Add the asparagus and blanch for 1–2 minutes.

2 Drain the asparagus, reserve and keep warm.

3 Heat the sunflower oil in a preheated wok or frying pan over a medium heat. Add the ginger, leek, carrots, and baby corn cobs and stir-fry for 3 minutes. Do not allow the vegetables to brown.

4 Add the soy sauce, oyster sauce and honey to the wok or frying pan.

5 Stir in the cooked shellfish and stir-fry for a further 2–3 minutes until the vegetables are just tender and the shellfish are thoroughly heated through. Add the blanched asparagus and stir-fry for about 2 minutes.

6 To serve, pile the cooked noodles on to 4 warmed serving plates and spoon the seafood and vegetable stir fry over them.

7 Garnish with the cooked prawns and snipped chives and serve.

SERVES 4

100 g/3½ oz small, thin asparagus spears, trimmed
1 tbsp sunflower oil
2.5-cm/1-inch piece of fresh root ginger, cut into thin strips
1 leek, shredded
2 carrots, cut into matchsticks
100 g/3½ oz baby corn cobs, quartered lengthways
2 tbsp light soy sauce
1 tbsp oyster sauce
1 tsp clear honey
450 g/1 lb cooked, assorted shellfish, thawed if frozen
freshly cooked egg noodles, to serve

to garnish
4 large, cooked prawns
small bunch of snipped fresh chives

NUTRITION
Calories *226*; Sugars *5 g*; Protein *35 g*;
Carbohydrate *6 g*; Fat *7 g*; Saturates *1 g*

 moderate

 5 mins

5 mins

15 mins

Delicately scented with sesame, lime and coriander, these noodles make an unusual lunch or supper dish.

Sesame Noodles *with* Prawns

SERVES 4

1 garlic clove, chopped
1 spring onion, chopped
1 small fresh red chilli, deseeded and sliced
1 tbsp chopped, fresh coriander
300 g/10½ oz dried fine egg noodles
2 tbsp vegetable oil
2 tsp sesame oil
1 tsp shrimp paste
225 g/8 oz raw prawns, peeled
2 tbsp lime juice
2 tbsp Thai fish sauce
1 tsp sesame seeds, toasted

1 Place the garlic, onion, chilli and coriander in a mortar and grind to a smooth paste with a pestle.

2 Bring a large saucepan of water to the boil over a medium heat. Add the noodles and cook for 4 minutes or according to the packet instructions.

3 Meanwhile, heat the oils in a preheated wok or large, heavy-based frying pan over a medium heat. Stir in the shrimp paste and ground coriander paste and stir-fry for 1 minute.

4 Add the prawns and stir-fry for 2 minutes. Stir in the lime juice and Thai fish sauce and cook for a further 1 minute.

5 Drain the noodles and add them to the wok, tossing well. Sprinkle with the sesame seeds and serve immediately.

NUTRITION

Calories *430*; Sugars *2 g*; Protein *23 g*; Carbohydrate *56 g*; Fat *15 g*; Saturates *3 g*

 easy

5 mins

10 mins

 **COOK'S TIP**

The roots of coriander are widely used in Thai cooking, so if you can buy fresh coriander with the root attached, the whole plant can be used in this dish for maximum flavour. If not, just use the stems and leaves.

This dish makes a delicious light lunch in a matter of minutes and would be a quick and easy mid-week supper accompanied by a crisp side salad.

Rice Noodles *with* Spinach

1 Soak the noodles in hot water for 15 minutes or according to the packet instructions, then drain well.

2 Soak the prawns in hot water for 10 minutes and drain. Wash the spinach, thoroughly, drain well and remove any tough stalks.

3 Heat the groundnut oil in a preheated wok or large frying pan over a medium heat. Add the garlic and stir-fry for 1 minute. Stir in the green curry paste and stir-fry for 30 seconds. Stir in the soaked prawns and stir-fry for 30 seconds.

4 Add the spinach and stir-fry for 1-2 minutes until the leaves are just wilted.

5 Stir in the sugar and soy sauce, then add the noodles and toss thoroughly to mix evenly. Transfer to 4 warmed serving bowls and serve immediately.

SERVES 4

115 g/4 oz thin rice stick noodles
2 tbsp dried prawns, optional
250 g/9 oz fresh young spinach
1 tbsp groundnut oil
2 garlic cloves, chopped finely
2 tsp Thai green curry paste
1 tsp sugar
1 tbsp light soy sauce

NUTRITION
Calories 159; Sugars 3 g; Protein 8 g;
Carbohydrate 27 g; Fat 2 g; Saturates 0 g

 easy

 20 mins

6–8 mins

🍲 **COOK'S TIP**

Young, tender spinach leaves, which cook in seconds are best for this dish. If you use older spinach shred the leaves before adding to the dish, so they cook more quickly.

This is the ideal dish when you have unexpected guests because the parcels are quick to prepare, but look fantastic.

Pasta *and* Prawn Parcels

SERVES 4

450 g/1 lb dried fettuccine
150 ml/5 fl oz pesto
4 tsp extra virgin olive oil
750 g/1 lb 10 oz large raw prawns, peeled and deveined
2 garlic cloves, crushed
125 ml/4 fl oz dry white wine
salt and pepper

1 Cut out four 30-cm/12-inch squares of greaseproof paper.

2 Bring a large saucepan of lightly salted water to the boil over a medium heat. Add the fettuccine and cook for 2–3 minutes until just softened. Drain and reserve.

3 Mix the fettuccine and half of the pesto together. Spread out the paper squares and put 1 teaspoon of olive oil in the centre of each. Divide the fettuccine between the squares, then divide the prawns and place on top of the fettuccine.

4 Mix the remaining pesto together with the garlic together and spoon it over the prawns. Season each parcel with salt and pepper and sprinkle with the wine.

5 Dampen the edges of the greaseproof paper and wrap the parcels loosely, twisting the edges to seal.

6 Place the parcels on a baking tray and bake them in a preheated oven, 200°C/400°F/Gas Mark 6, for 10–15 minutes. Transfer the parcels to 4 serving plates and serve immediately.

NUTRITION
Calories *640*; Sugars *1 g*; Protein *50 g*;
Carbohydrate *42 g*; Fat *29 g*; Saturates *4 g*

 moderate

15 mins

25 mins

COOK'S TIP

Traditionally, these parcels are designed to look like little money bags. The resemblance is more effective with greaseproof paper than with foil.

Fish and fruit are tossed with a trio of peppers in this spicy dish, which can be served with noodles for a quick, healthy meal.

Noodles *with* Cod *and* Mango

1 Place the egg noodles in a large bowl and pour over enough boiling water to cover. Leave to stand for about 10 minutes.

2 Place the cod in a large bowl, add the paprika and toss well to coat the fish.

3 Heat the sunflower oil in a preheated wok or large, heavy-based frying pan over a medium heat.

4 Add the onion, orange, red and green peppers and baby corn cobs to the wok and stir-fry for about 5 minutes.

5 Add the cod to the wok together with the sliced mango and stir-fry for a further 2–3 minutes or until the fish is tender.

6 Add the beansprouts to the wok and toss well to combine.

7 Mix the tomato ketchup, soy sauce, sherry and cornflour together. Add the mixture to the wok and cook, stirring occasionally, until the juices thicken.

8 Drain the noodles well and transfer to 4 warmed serving bowls. Transfer the cod and mango stir-fry to separate serving bowls. Serve immediately.

SERVES 4

250 g/9 oz dried egg noodles
450 g/1 lb skinless cod fillet,
   cut into thin strips
1 tbsp paprika
2 tbsp sunflower oil
1 red onion, sliced
1 orange pepper, deseeded and sliced
1 red pepper, deseeded and sliced
1 green pepper, deseeded and sliced
100 g/3½ oz baby corn cobs,
   halved lengthways
1 mango, peeled, stoned and sliced
100 g/3½ oz beansprouts
2 tbsp tomato ketchup
2 tbsp soy sauce
2 tbsp medium sherry
1 tsp cornflour

NUTRITION
Calories *274*; Sugars *11 g*; Protein *25 g*;
Carbohydrate *26 g*; Fat *8 g*; Saturates *1 g*

 moderate

 10 mins

🕐 25 mins

This is another tempting seafood dish where the eye is delighted as much as the taste buds.

Baked Scallops *with* Pasta *in* Shells

SERVES 4

12 scallops
2 tbsp olive oil
350 g/12 oz small, dried wholemeal
    pasta shells
150 ml/5 fl oz fish stock
1 onion, chopped
juice and finely grated rind of 2 lemons
150 ml/5 fl oz double cream
225 g/8 oz grated Cheddar cheese
salt and pepper

to serve
lime wedges
crusty brown bread

NUTRITION
Calories 725; Sugars 2 g; Protein 38 g;
Carbohydrate 38 g; Fat 48 g; Saturates 25 g

 moderate

 20 mins

20 mins

30 mins

1 Very carefully ease the scallops from their shells with a short, but very strong knife, and rinse them to remove any sand. Scrape off the skirt and the black intestinal thread. Reserve the white part (the flesh) and the orange part (the coral or roe).

2 Wash the shells under cold running water and dry them with kitchen paper. Put the shells on to a baking tray, sprinkle with about two-thirds of the olive oil and reserve.

3 Meanwhile, bring a pan of lightly salted water to the boil over a medium heat. Add the pasta and 1 teaspoon of oil and cook until tender, but still firm to the bite. Drain and spoon 25 g/1 oz of pasta into each scallop shell.

4 Put the scallops, fish stock and onion into a large ovenproof dish and season with pepper to taste. Cover with foil and bake in a preheated oven, 180°C/350°F/Gas Mark 4, for 8 minutes.

5 Remove from the oven, remove the foil, then use a slotted spoon to transfer the scallops to the shells. Add 1 tablespoon of the cooking liquid to each shell, together with a drizzle of lemon juice, a little lemon rind and cream, and top with the Cheddar cheese.

6 Increase the oven temperature to 230°C/450°F/Gas Mark 8 and return the scallops to the oven for a further 4 minutes.

7 Serve the scallops in their shells with lime wedges and crusty brown bread.

Brill was once known as poor man's turbot, an unfair description as it is a delicately flavoured and delicious fish in its own right.

Spaghetti *alla* Bucaniera

1 Season the flour with salt and pepper, then sprinkle 3 tablespoons of the seasoned flour on to a shallow plate. Press the fish pieces into the seasoned flour until they are thoroughly coated.

2 Melt the butter in a flameproof casserole over a low heat. Add the fish fillets, shallots, garlic, carrot and leek and cook, stirring frequently, for about 10 minutes.

3 Sprinkle over the remaining seasoned flour and cook, stirring constantly, for 2 minutes. Gradually stir in the cider, anchovy essence and tarragon vinegar. Bring the mixture to the boil and simmer for 35 minutes. Alternatively, bake in a preheated oven, 180°C/350°F/Gas Mark 4, for about 30 minutes.

4 About 15 minutes before the end of the cooking time, bring a large saucepan of lightly salted water to the boil over a medium heat. Add the spaghetti and olive oil and cook for about 12 minutes or until tender, but still firm to the bite. Drain well and transfer to a large serving dish.

5 Arrange the fish on top of the spaghetti and pour over the sauce. Garnish with chopped parsley and serve immediately.

SERVES 4

85 g/3 oz plain flour
450 g/1 lb brill or sole fillets,
    skinned and chopped
450 g/1 lb hake fillets, skinned and chopped
6 tbsp butter
4 shallots, chopped finely
2 garlic cloves, crushed
1 carrot, diced
1 leek, chopped finely
300 ml/10 fl oz dry cider
300 ml/10 fl oz medium sweet cider
2 tsp anchovy essence
1 tbsp tarragon vinegar
450 g/1 lb dried spaghetti
1 tsp olive oil
salt and pepper
chopped fresh parsley, to garnish

NUTRITION
Calories *588*; Sugars *5 g*; Protein *36 g*;
Carbohydrate *68 g*; Fat *18 g*; Saturates *9 g*

   moderate

25 mins

50 mins

🍳 COOK'S TIP

Flavoured vinegars are easy to make. Simply place a few sprigs of fresh herbs into a bottle of white wine vinegar. Screw down tightly and leave in a cool dark place for 2–3 weeks before using.

This quick, easy and inexpensive dish would be ideal for an everyday family supper, as it is both nourishing and filling.

Smoked Haddock Casserole

S E R V E S 4

2 tbsp butter, plus extra for greasing
450 g/1 lb smoked haddock fillets,
  cut into 4 slices
600 ml/1 pint milk
2½ tbsp plain flour
pinch of freshly grated nutmeg
3 tbsp double cream
1 tbsp chopped fresh parsley
2 eggs, hard-boiled and mashed to a pulp
450 g/1 lb dried fusilli
1 tbsp lemon juice
salt and pepper
fresh flat-leaved parsley sprigs, to garnish

to serve
boiled new potatoes
freshly cooked beetroot

N U T R I T I O N
Calories *525*; Sugars *8 g*; Protein *41 g*;
Carbohydrate *53 g*; Fat *18 g*; Saturates *10 g*

  moderate
  20 mins
  45 mins

1 Thoroughly grease a casserole with a little butter. Put the haddock into the casserole and pour over the milk. Bake in a preheated oven, 200°C/400°F/Gas Mark 6, for about 15 minutes until tender and the flesh flakes easily.

2 Carefully pour the cooking liquid into a jug without breaking up the fish. Leave the fish in the casserole.

3 Melt the butter in a small saucepan over a low heat. Stir in the flour, then gradually whisk in the reserved cooking liquid. Season to taste with salt, pepper and nutmeg. Stir in the cream, parsley and mashed hard-boiled eggs and cook, stirring constantly, for 2 minutes.

4 Meanwhile, bring a large saucepan of lightly salted water to the boil over a medium heat. Add the fusilli and lemon juice, bring back to the boil and cook for 8–10 minutes until tender, but still firm to the bite.

5 Drain the pasta and spoon or tip it over the fish. Top with the egg sauce and return the casserole to the oven for 10 minutes.

6 Transfer the casserole to 4 large, warmed serving plates, garnish with a few sprigs of fresh parsley and serve with boiled new potatoes and beetroot.

C O O K ' S T I P

You can use any type of dried pasta for this casserole. Try penne, conchiglie, farfalle or rigatoni.

This dish is ideal for a substantial supper. You can use whatever pasta you like, but the tricolour varieties will give the most colourful results.

Prawn Pasta Bake

1 Bring a large saucepan of lightly salted water to the boil over a medium heat. Add the pasta, bring back to the boil and cook for 8–10 minutes until tender, but still firm to the bite. Drain well.

2 Meanwhile, heat the vegetable oil in a large frying pan over a low heat. Add the mushrooms and all but a handful of the spring onions and cook, stirring occasionally, for 4–5 minutes until softened.

3 Place the cooked pasta in a large bowl and stir in the mushroom mixture, tuna and prawns.

4 Blend the cornflour with a little milk to make a paste. Pour the remaining milk into a saucepan and stir in the paste. Heat, stirring constantly, until the sauce begins to thicken. Season well with salt and pepper. Stir the sauce into the pasta mixture. Transfer to an ovenproof dish and place on a baking tray.

5 Arrange the tomato slices over the pasta and sprinkle with the breadcrumbs and cheese. Bake in a preheated oven, 190°C/375°F/Gas Mark 5, for about 25–30 minutes until golden. Sprinkle with the reserved spring onions and serve immediately.

SERVES 4

225 g/8 oz tricolour pasta shapes
1 tbsp vegetable oil
175 g/6 oz button mushrooms, sliced
1 bunch of spring onions, trimmed and chopped
400 g/14 oz canned tuna in brine, drained and flaked
175 g/6 oz cooked peeled prawns, thawed if frozen
2 tbsp cornflour
425 ml/15 fl oz skimmed milk
4 medium tomatoes, sliced thinly
25 g/1 oz fresh breadcrumbs
25 g/1 oz reduced-fat Cheddar cheese, grated
salt and pepper

NUTRITION
Calories 723; Sugars 9 g; Protein 56 g; Carbohydrate 114 g; Fat 8 g; Saturates 2 g

 challenging

 10 mins

50 mins

Entertaining

Fish and shellfish are ideal for entertaining. They are perceived to be more exotic than many meat dishes and yet are often easier to prepare. Shellfish in particular is thought to be luxurious, but nowadays it is readily available and reasonably priced.

The recipes in this chapter have been designed for those occasions when you really want to make an impression. There should be something here for every budget, ability and taste, from Stuffed Monkfish Tail, and Crab Soufflé, to Hot-smoked Trout Tart, and Spinach Roulade.

There are more traditional dishes, such as Luxury Fish Pie and Sole Florentine, as well as more exciting-sounding dishes like Cuttlefish in Their Own Ink.

Skate has a strong flavour that makes it a rich fish. It is perfect partnered with this sauce, which is sharp in flavour. Serve it with boiled new potatoes and a green vegetable, such as French beans.

Skate *with* Black Butter

SERVES 4

900 g/2 lb skate wings, cut into 4 pieces
175 g/6 oz butter
50 ml/2 fl oz red wine vinegar
15 g/½ oz capers, drained
1 tbsp chopped fresh parsley
salt and pepper

court-bouillon

850 ml/1½ pints cold water
850 ml/1½ pints dry white wine
3 tbsp white wine vinegar
2 large carrots, chopped roughly
1 onion, chopped roughly
2 celery sticks, chopped roughly
2 leeks, chopped roughly
2 garlic cloves, chopped roughly
2 bay leaves
4 fresh parsley sprigs
4 fresh thyme sprigs
6 black peppercorns

to serve

boiled new potatoes
freshly cooked French beans

NUTRITION

Calories *381*; Sugars *0 g*; Protein *34 g*;
Carbohydrate *0 g*; Fat *27 g*; Saturates *17 g*

easy

20 mins

1 hr 30 mins

1 Begin by making the court-bouillon. Put all of the ingredients into a large saucepan, together with 1 teaspoon of salt and bring slowly to the boil over a low heat. Cover and simmer gently for 30 minutes. Strain the liquid through a fine sieve into a clean pan. Bring to the boil again and simmer rapidly, uncovered, for 15–20 minutes, until reduced to 600 ml/1 pint.

2 Place the skate in a wide shallow pan and pour over the court-bouillon. Bring to the boil over a low heat and simmer very gently for 15 minutes, or a little longer depending on the thickness of the skate. Drain the fish, reserve and keep warm.

3 Meanwhile, melt the butter in a frying pan over a medium heat. Cook until the butter changes colour to a dark brown and smells very nutty.

4 Add the vinegar, capers and parsley and simmer for 1 minute. Pour over the fish. Serve with plenty of boiled new potatoes and French beans.

Dover sole à la Meunière, or 'miller's wife style', gets its name from the light dusting of flour that the fish is given before frying.

Dover Sole *à la* Meunière

1 Mix the flour with the salt and place on a large plate or tray. Drop the fish into the flour, one at a time, and shake well to remove any excess. Melt 40 g/1½ oz of the butter in a small saucepan over a low heat and use to liberally brush the fish all over.

2 Put the fish under a preheated hot grill and cook for 5 minutes on each side.

3 Meanwhile, melt the remaining butter in a pan over a low heat. Pour cold water into a bowl, large enough to take the base of the pan. Keep nearby.

4 Heat the butter until it turns golden brown and begins to smell nutty. Remove immediately from the heat and immerse the base of the pan in the cold water to stop cooking.

5 Put the fish on to 4 large serving plates, drizzle with the lemon juice and sprinkle with the parsley and preserved lemon (if using). Pour over the browned butter and garnish with a few sprigs of fresh parsley and lemon wedges. Serve immediately.

SERVES 4

50 g/1¾ oz plain flour
1 tsp salt
4 Dover soles, about 400 g/14 oz each, cleaned and skinned
150 g/5½ oz butter
3 tbsp lemon juice
1 tbsp chopped fresh parsley
¼ of a preserved lemon, chopped finely (optional)

to garnish
fresh parsley sprigs
lemon wedges

NUTRITION
Calories *584*; Sugars *0 g*; Protein *74 g*; Carbohydrate *10 g*; Fat *29 g*; Saturates *14 g*

★★ easy
20 mins
15 mins

🍴 **COOK'S TIP**

If you have a large enough frying pan you can fry the floured fish in butter, if you prefer.

This is a classic combination of rolled sole fillets in a creamy cheese sauce cooked with spinach. To save time, prepare the cheese sauce in advance.

Sole Florentine

SERVES 4

600 ml/1 pint milk
2 strips of lemon rind
2 fresh tarragon sprigs
1 bay leaf
½ onion, sliced
50 g/1¾ oz butter, plus extra for greasing
50 g/1¾ oz plain flour
2 tsp mustard powder
25 g/1 oz freshly grated Parmesan cheese
300 ml/10 fl oz double cream
pinch of freshly grated nutmeg
450 g/1 lb fresh spinach, washed
4 Dover sole, quarter-cut fillets (2 from
    each side of the fish), about 750 g/
    1 lb 10 oz each
salt and pepper
crisp green salad, to serve

NUTRITION

Calories *945*; Sugars *12 g*; Protein *80 g*;
Carbohydrate *23 g*; Fat *59 g*; Saturates *32 g*

moderate

45 mins

45 mins

1 Put the milk, lemon rind, tarragon, bay leaf and onion into a saucepan and bring slowly to the boil over a low heat. Remove from the heat and leave to stand for 30 minutes.

2 Melt the butter in a clean saucepan over a low heat. Stir in the flour and mustard powder until smooth. Strain the infused milk, discarding the lemon, herbs and onion. Gradually beat the milk into the butter and flour mixture until smooth. Bring slowly to the boil, stirring, until thickened. Cook for 2 minutes. Remove from the heat and stir in the Parmesan cheese, cream, nutmeg and seasoning. Cover with clingfilm and reserve.

3 Lightly grease a large baking dish. Bring a saucepan of water to the boil over a medium heat. Add the spinach leaves and blanch for 30 seconds. Drain and refresh under cold running water. Drain and pat dry with kitchen paper. Put the spinach in a layer on the base of the prepared dish.

4 Wash the fish under cold running water and pat dry with kitchen paper. Season to taste with salt and pepper and roll up. Arrange on top of the spinach and pour over the sauce. Bake in a preheated oven, 200°C/400°F/Gas Mark 6, for 35 minutes until bubbling and golden. Serve with a green salad.

COOK'S TIP

For a budget version of this dish, use lemon sole instead of Dover sole.

The beauty of this dish is that the fish cooks alongside a selection of vegetables, which means you need only boil some new potatoes to serve with it.

John Dory *en* Papillote

1 Wash the fish fillets under cold running water and pat dry with kitchen paper, then reserve. Cut 4 large rectangles of baking parchment measuring about 46 x 30 cm/18 x 12 inches. Fold each in half to give a 23 x 30 cm/9 x 12 inch rectangle. Cut this into a large heart shape and open out.

2 Lay 1 John Dory fillet on one half of each paper heart. Top with one quarter of the olives, tomatoes, green beans and basil and 1 lemon slice. Drizzle over 1 teaspoon of olive oil and season well with salt and pepper.

3 Fold over the other half of the paper and then fold the edges of the paper together to enclose. Repeat to make 4 parcels.

4 Place the parcels on a baking sheet and cook in a preheated oven, 200°C/400°F/Gas Mark 6, for 15 minutes or until the fish is tender.

5 Transfer each parcel to a serving plate, unopened, allowing your guests to open their parcels and enjoy the wonderful aroma. Suggest that they garnish their portions with fresh basil and serve with a generous helping of boiled new potatoes.

SERVES 4

2 John Dory, filleted
115 g/4 oz stoned black olives
12 cherry tomatoes, halved
115 g/4 oz green beans, trimmed
handful of fresh basil leaves
4 lemon slices
4 tsp olive oil
salt and pepper
fresh basil leaves, to garnish
boiled new potatoes, to serve

 COOK'S TIP

Try spreading the fish with a little olive paste, some chopped sun-dried tomatoes, a little goat's cheese and fresh basil.

NUTRITION
Calories *368*; Sugars *2 g*; Protein *49 g*;
Carbohydrate *3 g*; Fat *18 g*; Saturates *3 g*

easy

10 mins

15 mins

Baby artichokes are slowly cooked with olive oil, garlic, thyme and lemon to create a soft blend of flavours that harmonise very well with the fish, without overpowering it.

Grilled Sea Bass *with* Artichokes

SERVES 4

1.7 kg/4 lb baby artichokes
2½ tbsp fresh lemon juice, plus the cut halves of the lemon
150 ml/5 fl oz olive oil
10 garlic cloves, sliced finely
1 tbsp fresh thyme plus extra, to garnish
6 sea bass fillets, about 115 g/4 oz each
1 tbsp olive oil
salt and pepper
crusty bread, to serve

1 Peel away the tough outer leaves of each artichoke until the yellow-green heart is revealed. Slice off the pointed top at about halfway between the point and the top of the stem. Cut off the stem and pare off what is left of the dark green leaves surrounding the bottom of the artichoke.

2 Submerge the prepared artichokes in water containing the cut halves of the lemon to prevent them browning. When all the artichokes have been prepared, turn them choke-side down and slice thinly.

3 Warm the olive oil in a large saucepan over a low heat. Add the artichokes, garlic, thyme, lemon juice and salt and pepper to taste. Cover and cook the artichokes for 20–30 minutes, without colouring, until tender.

4 Meanwhile, brush the sea bass fillets with the remaining olive oil and season well with salt and pepper. Transfer to a lit barbecue or preheated ridged griddle pan and cook for 3–4 minutes on each side until just tender.

5 Divide the stewed artichokes between 4 serving plates and top each with a sea bass fillet. Garnish with chopped thyme and serve with crusty bread.

NUTRITION
Calories *400*; Sugars *3 g*; Protein *28 g*;
Carbohydrate *7 g*; Fat *30 g*; Saturates *5 g*

 easy

20 mins

35 mins

 **COOK'S TIP**

If fresh artichokes are unavailable, use canned.

Sea bass is surely the king of round fish, with a delightful flavour and texture. Here it is cooked very simply and served with a highly flavoured sauce of ratatouille and a basil dressing.

Sea Bass *with* Ratatouille

1 To make the ratatouille, cut the aubergine and courgettes into chunks about the same size as the onion and peppers. Put the aubergine and courgette into a colander with the salt and leave to drain for 30 minutes. Rinse thoroughly and pat dry on kitchen paper. Reserve.

2 Heat the olive oil in a large saucepan over a low heat. Add the onion and garlic and cook gently for 10 minutes until softened. Add the peppers, aubergine and courgettes. Season to taste with salt and pepper and stir well. Cover and simmer very gently for 30 minutes until all the vegetables have softened. Add the tomatoes and cook for a further 15 minutes.

3 Meanwhile, make the dressing. Put the basil, garlic, and half the olive oil into a food processor and process until finely chopped. Add the remaining olive oil and lemon juice and season to taste with salt and pepper.

4 Season the sea bass fillets with salt and pepper and brush with a little olive oil. Preheat a frying pan until very hot and add the fish, skin side down. Cook for 2–3 minutes until the skin is browned and crispy. Turn the fish and cook for a further 2–3 minutes until just cooked through.

5 To serve, stir the basil into the ratatouille, then transfer to 4 serving plates. Top with the fresh fried fish and spoon around the dressing, then serve.

SERVES 4

2 large sea bass, filleted
2 tbsp olive oil, for brushing
salt and pepper

ratatouille
1 large aubergine
2 medium courgettes
1 tbsp sea salt
4 tbsp olive oil
1 medium onion, chopped roughly
2 garlic cloves, crushed
½ red pepper, deseeded and
    roughly chopped
½ green pepper, deseeded and
    roughly chopped
2 large ripe tomatoes, peeled and chopped
1 tbsp chopped fresh basil

dressing
5 tbsp chopped roughly fresh basil
2 garlic cloves, chopped roughly
4 tbsp olive oil
1 tbsp lemon juice

NUTRITION
Calories 373; Sugars 9 g; Protein 42 g;
Carbohydrate 10 g; Fat 18 g; Saturates 3 g

moderate

45 mins

1 hr

This is a lovely oriental-inspired dish of sea bass, delicately flavoured with spring onions, ginger and soy sauce. Be careful when pouring the hot oil over the fish and spring onions, as it may spit a little.

Whole Sea Bass *with* Ginger

SERVES 4

800 g/1 lb 12 oz whole sea bass, scaled and gutted
4 tbsp light soy sauce
5 spring onions, cut into long, fine shreds
2 tbsp finely shredded fresh root ginger
4 tbsp fresh coriander leaves
5 tsp sunflower oil
1 tsp sesame oil
4 tbsp hot fish stock
lime wedges, to garnish
steamed rice, to serve

1 Wash the sea bass under cold running water and pat dry with kitchen paper. Brush with 2 tablespoons of the soy sauce. Scatter half the spring onions and all the ginger over a steaming tray or large plate and put the fish on top.

2 Half fill a large saucepan with water and fit a steamer on top. Bring the water to the boil over a medium heat. Put the steaming plate with the sea bass into the steamer and cover with a tight-fitting lid. Keeping the water boiling, steam the fish for 10–12 minutes until tender.

3 Carefully remove the plate and lift the fish on to a serving plate, leaving behind the spring onions and ginger. Scatter over the remaining spring onions and coriander leaves.

4 Put the sunflower oil into a small saucepan and heat until almost smoking. Add the sesame oil and immediately pour over the fish and spring onions. Mix the remaining soy sauce with the fish stock, then pour over the fish. Garnish with lime wedges and serve immediately with steamed rice .

NUTRITION
Calories *185*; Sugars *1 g*; Protein *31 g*; Carbohydrate *2 g*; Fat *6 g*; Saturates *1 g*

moderate

10 mins

15 mins

Poached cod has a very delicate flavour. Here it is teamed with a piquant relish of finely diced, colourful vegetables, both served cold.

Cold Poached Cod Steaks

1 Put the carrot, onion, celery, parsley, thyme, garlic, water and 1 teaspoon of salt into a large saucepan and bring to the boil over a medium heat. Simmer gently for 10 minutes. Add the fish and poach for 5–7 minutes until just firm in the centre. Remove the fish with a slotted spoon and leave to cool. Leave to chill in the refrigerator for 2 hours.

2 Meanwhile, make the pickled vegetable relish. Soak the salted anchovies in several changes of water for 15 minutes, then chop. Mix the carrot, red pepper, red onion, garlic, cornichons, olives, capers, anchovies, vinegar, olive oil and parsley together in a non-metallic bowl. Season to taste with salt and pepper, adding a little more vinegar or olive oil to taste. Cover and leave to chill in the refrigerator for 1 hour.

3 To serve, place a cold cod steak on each of 4 serving plates. Spoon the relish over the top. Serve immediately with salad leaves.

 COOK'S TIP

You can also use salmon steaks for this dish, if you prefer.

SERVES 4

1 small carrot, sliced thinly
1 small onion, sliced thinly
1 celery stick, sliced thinly
3 fresh parsley sprigs
3 fresh thyme sprigs
1 garlic clove, sliced
1.7 litres/3 pints water
4 cod steaks, about 175 g/6 oz each

pickled vegetable relish
2 salted anchovies
1 small carrot, diced finely
¼ red pepper, deseeded and finely diced
½ small red onion, diced finely
1 garlic clove, chopped finely
3 tbsp diced finely cornichon pickles
4 tbsp chopped stoned green olives
1 tbsp capers, drained and rinsed
1 tbsp red wine vinegar
100 ml/3½ fl oz olive oil
2 tbsp chopped fresh parsley
salt and pepper
salad leaves, to serve

NUTRITION
Calories *402*; Sugars *3 g*; Protein *33 g*;
Carbohydrate *4 g*; Fat *28 g*; Saturates *4 g*

 moderate

2hrs 30 mins

7 mins

Cooking the fish in a layer of salt ensures that the flesh stays very moist without becoming salty.

Sea Bream *in a* Salt Crust

SERVES 4

1 kg/2 lb 4 oz whole sea bream
1 shallot, sliced thinly
2 fresh parsley sprigs
1 fresh tarragon sprig
2 garlic cloves, chopped roughly
2–2.5 kg/4 lb 8 oz–5 lb 8 oz coarse sea salt

lemon butter sauce

2 shallots, very finely chopped
4 tbsp lemon juice
300 g/10½ oz cold unsalted butter, diced
salt and pepper

to garnish

lemon wedges
fresh herb sprigs

NUTRITION
Calories *185*; Sugars *1 g*; Protein *31 g*;
Carbohydrate *2 g*; Fat *6 g*; Saturates *1 g*

 moderate

 10 mins

10 mins

25 mins

1 Wash the sea bream under cold running water and pat dry with kitchen paper. Stuff the body cavity with the shallot, parsley, tarragon and garlic, then reserve.

2 Sprinkle a thick layer of salt into the base of a roasting tin large enough to hold the fish, with lots of space round it. Top with the fish, then pour the remaining salt over the fish to completely cover it. Sprinkle the water lightly all over the salt. Cook in a preheated oven, 220°C/425°F/Gas Mark 7, for about 25 minutes.

3 To make the lemon butter sauce, put the shallots and lemon juice into a saucepan and simmer gently over a low heat for 5 minutes. Increase the heat until the lemon juice is reduced by half. Reduce the heat and add the butter, piece by piece, whisking constantly, until all the butter is incorporated and the sauce is thick. Season to taste with salt and pepper and keep warm.

4 Remove the fish from the oven and leave to stand for 5 minutes before cracking open the salt. Remove the fish, garnish with lemon wedges and fresh herbs and serve with the lemon butter sauce.

COOK'S TIP

Use unscented pure bath salts, if you can find them, rather than the more expensive salt for the table.

This is a dramatic looking dish due to the inclusion of the cuttlefish ink. Although this is a typically Spanish dish, it has been teamed with polenta as the combination of the dark stew and yellow polenta make a beautiful contrast.

Cuttlefish *in Their Own* Ink

1 To prepare the cuttlefish, cut off the tentacles in front of the eyes and remove the beak-like mouth from the centre of the tentacles. Cut the head section from the body and discard it. Cut open the body section from top to bottom along the dark-coloured back. Remove the cuttle bone and the entrails, reserving the ink sac. Skin the body. Chop the flesh roughly and reserve. Split open the ink sac and dilute the ink in a little water. Reserve.

2 Heat the oil in a large saucepan over a low heat. Add the onion and cook gently for 8–10 minutes until softened and beginning to brown. Add the garlic and cook for a further 30 seconds. Add the reserved cuttlefish and cook for a further 5 minutes until beginning to brown. Add the paprika and stir for a further 30 seconds before adding the tomatoes. Cook for about 2–3 minutes until the tomatoes have collapsed.

3 Add the red wine, fish stock and diluted ink and stir well. Bring to the boil and simmer gently, uncovered, for 25 minutes until the cuttlefish is tender and the sauce has thickened. Season to taste with salt and pepper.

4 Meanwhile, cook the polenta according to the packet instructions. When cooked, remove from the heat, stir in the parsley and season to taste with salt and pepper.

5 Transfer the polenta to 4 serving plates and top with the cuttlefish and its sauce. Garnish with a few sprigs of fresh herbs and serve.

SERVES 4

450 g/1 lb small cuttlefish, with their ink (or substitute squid)
4 tbsp olive oil
1 small onion, chopped finely
2 garlic cloves, chopped finely
1 tsp paprika, preferably Spanish
175 g/6 oz ripe tomatoes, peeled, deseeded and chopped
150 ml/5 fl oz red wine
150 ml/5 fl oz fish stock
225 g/8 oz instant polenta
3 tbsp chopped fresh flat-leaved parsley
salt and pepper
fresh herb sprigs, to garnish

NUTRITION
Calories *430*; Sugars *2 g*; Protein *24 g*; Carbohydrate *44 g*; Fat *14 g*; Saturates *2 g*

 moderate

 20 mins

20 mins

25 mins

This is an interesting and elegant way of presenting an ordinary salmon steak.

Noisettes *of* Salmon

SERVES 4

4 salmon steaks
50 g/1¾ oz butter, softened
1 garlic clove, crushed
2 tsp mustard seeds
2 tbsp chopped fresh thyme
1 tbsp chopped fresh parsley
2 tbsp vegetable oil
4 tomatoes, peeled, deseeded and chopped
salt and pepper

to serve
boiled new potatoes
green vegetables or salad

1 Carefully remove the central bone from the salmon steaks and cut them in half. Curl each piece around to form a medallion and tie with string. Blend the butter, garlic, mustard seeds, thyme, parsley and seasoning together and reserve.

2 Heat the vegetable oil in a preheated ridged griddle pan or large frying pan over a medium heat. Add the salmon noisettes and brown on both sides, in batches, if necessary. Drain on kitchen paper and leave to cool.

3 Cut 4 pieces of baking paper into 30-cm/12-inch squares. Place 2 salmon noisettes on top of each square and top with a little of the flavoured butter and chopped tomato. Draw up the edges of the paper and fold together to enclose the fish. Place on a baking sheet.

4 Cook in a preheated oven, 200°C/400°F/Gas Mark 6, for 10–15 minutes or until the salmon is cooked through. Serve immediately while still warm with boiled new potatoes and a green vegetable or salad of your choice.

NUTRITION

Calories *381*; Sugars *3 g*; Protein *36 g*; Carbohydrate *3 g*; Fat *26 g*; Saturates *4 g*

 moderate

20 mins

25 mins

COOK'S TIP

You can make cod steaks into noisettes in the same way. Cook them with butter flavoured with chives and basil.

Although the fish is quite simple to cook, a whole salmon always makes a very impressive centrepiece for any party.

Whole Poached Salmon

1 Wash the salmon under cold running water and pat dry with kitchen paper, then remove the fins. Place the salmon in a fish kettle or large, heavy-based roasting tin. Pour over the court-bouillon. Bring slowly to the boil over a low heat. As soon as the liquid comes to a simmer, remove from the heat and leave to go cold.

2 Meanwhile, make the watercress mayonnaise. Put the egg yolk, garlic, mustard, lemon juice, watercress and basil into a food processor and process until the herbs are very finely chopped. Gradually add the olive oil, drop by drop, until the mixture begins to thicken. Continue adding the olive oil in a steady stream until it all the oil is incorporated. Transfer to a bowl and add the spring onion. Season to taste with salt and pepper and leave to chill in the refrigerator until required.

3 When the salmon is cold, carefully lift it from the poaching liquid and pat dry with kitchen paper. Carefully peel away and discard the skin from the rounder, uppermost side, then turn the fish and remove the skin from the flatter underside. Slide a knife along the backbone of the fish to remove the flesh in 1 piece. Turn it over on to the serving platter so it is cut side is up.

4 Remove the bones from the remaining piece of fish, then turn the remaining flesh on top of the first piece to reform the fish. Place the head and tail back on the fish to make it appear whole. Lay the cucumber on top of the fish, starting at the tail end, in a pattern resembling scales. Serve with the mayonnaise.

SERVES 4 – 6

1.5 kg/3 lb 5 oz salmon, scaled and gutted
3 x quantity Court-Bouillon (see page 150)
½ cucumber, sliced very thinly

watercress mayonnaise
1 egg yolk
1 garlic clove, crushed
1 tsp Dijon mustard
1 tbsp lemon juice
50 g/1¾ oz watercress leaves, chopped roughly
1 tbsp chopped fresh basil
225 ml/8 fl oz light olive oil
1 spring onion, chopped finely
salt and pepper

NUTRITION
Calories *661*; Sugars *1 g*; Protein *35 g*;
Carbohydrate *1 g*; Fat *57 g*; Saturates *9 g*

 moderate

1 hr 15 mins

10 mins

This is a very impressive looking dish which is very simple to prepare. Serve with stir-fried vegetables and boiled new potatoes.

Stuffed Monkfish Tail

SERVES 6

750 g/1 lb 10 oz monkfish tail, skinned and trimmed
6 slices Parma ham
4 tbsp chopped mixed herbs such as parsley, chives, basil and sage
1 tsp finely grated lemon rind
2 tbsp olive oil
salt and pepper

to serve

shredded stir-fried vegetables
boiled new potatoes

1 Using a sharp knife, carefully cut down each side of the central bone of the monkfish to leave 2 fillets. Wash the fillets under cold running water and pat dry with kitchen paper.

2 Lay the Parma ham slices widthways on a clean work surface so that they overlap slightly. Lay the fish fillets lengthways on top of the ham so that the 2 cut sides face each other.

3 Mix the chopped herbs and lemon rind together. Season well with salt and pepper. Pack this mixture on to the cut surface of 1 monkfish fillet. Press the 2 fillets together and wrap tightly with the Parma ham slices. Secure with string or cocktail sticks.

4 Heat the olive oil in a large, heavy-based frying pan over a low heat. Place the fish in the pan, seam side down first, and brown the wrapped monkfish tail all over.

5 Transfer the fish to a large, ovenproof dish and cook in a preheated oven, 200°C/400°F/Gas Mark 6, for 25 minutes until golden and the fish is tender. Remove from the oven and leave to rest for 10 minutes before slicing thickly. Serve with shredded stir-fried vegetables and new potatoes.

NUTRITION

Calories *154*; Sugars *0 g*; Protein *24 g*; Carbohydrate *0 g*; Fat *6 g*; Saturates *1 g*

⭐⭐⭐ moderate

🕐 30 mins

🕐 25 mins

  COOK'S TIP

It is possible to remove the central bone from a monkfish tail without separating the 2 fillets. This makes it easier to stuff, but takes some practice.

You could cook the lobsters on the barbecue, if you prefer. Place them shell-side down, to protect the meat from the fierce heat of the fire and grill until nearly ready then turn briefly flesh-side down.

Grilled Lobster *with* Beurre Blanc

1 Put the lobsters into the freezer for about 2 hours, then take a very large knife and cleave them in 2, lengthways behind the head. Dot the lobster flesh with the butter. Transfer to a grill pan and cook, flesh side up, under a preheated very hot grill for 5–7 minutes until the flesh of the lobster becomes firm and opaque.

2 Meanwhile, put the shallots into a small saucepan with the vinegar, white wine and water. Bring to the boil over a medium–low heat and simmer until only 1 tablespoon of liquid remains. Reduce the heat to low and begin adding the butter, one piece at a time, whisking constantly. Add the next piece of butter when the last bit has been incorporated and continue until all the butter is used and the sauce has thickened.

3 Stir in the tarragon and parsley and season to taste with salt and pepper.

4 Transfer the lobster to 4 serving plates and spoon over the beurre blanc. Garnish with lemon wedges and a few sprigs of fresh parsley and serve.

SERVES 4

4 live lobsters, about 450 g/1 lb each
25 g/1 oz butter

beurre blanc
25 g/1 oz shallots, chopped finely
1 tbsp white wine vinegar
1 tbsp dry white wine
50 ml/2 fl oz water
150 g/5½ oz cold unsalted butter, diced
2 tsp chopped fresh tarragon
1 tbsp chopped fresh parsley
salt and pepper

to garnish
lemon wedges
fresh parsley sprigs

NUTRITION
Calories *499*; Sugars *0.5 g*; Protein *36 g*;
Carbohydrate *1 g*; Fat *39 g*; Saturates *24 g*

 moderate

2 hrs 15 mins

10 mins

👑 COOK'S TIP

There is controversy about the most humane way to kill a lobster. The RSPCA has suggested that putting the lobsters in a freezer for 2 hours before cooking them will kill them painlessly.

This isn't really a main course dish but it would serve very well as a light lunch with some bread or as part of a buffet.

Lobster *and* Avocado Salad

S E R V E S 4

2 cooked lobsters, about 400 g/14 oz each
1 large, ripe avocado
1 tbsp lemon juice
225 g/8 oz green beans
4 spring onions, sliced thinly
2 tbsp chopped fresh chervil
1 tbsp snipped fresh chives

dressing
1 garlic clove, crushed
1 tsp Dijon mustard
pinch of sugar
1 tbsp balsamic vinegar
5 tbsp olive oil
salt and pepper

N U T R I T I O N
Calories *313*; Sugars *3 g*; Protein *19 g*;
Carbohydrate *4 g*; Fat *25 g*; Saturates *4 g*

easy

25 mins

3 mins

1 To prepare the lobsters, cut them in half lengthways. Remove the intestinal vein that runs down the tail, stomach sac and any grey beards from the body cavity at the head end of the lobster. Crack the claws and remove the meat – in one piece if possible. Remove the meat from the tail of each lobster. Roughly chop all the meat and reserve.

2 Split the avocado lengthways and remove the stone. Cut each half in half again and peel away the skin. Cut the avocado into chunks and toss with the lemon juice. Add to the lobster meat.

3 Bring a large saucepan of lightly salted water to the boil over a medium heat. Add the beans and cook for 3 minutes, then drain and immediately refresh under cold water. Drain again and leave to go completely cold. Cut the beans in half, then add to the avocado and lobster.

4 Meanwhile, make the dressing by whisking the garlic, mustard, sugar, vinegar and seasoning together in a bowl. Gradually add the olive oil, whisking, until thickened.

5 Add the spring onions, chervil and chives to the lobster and avocado mixture and toss gently together. Drizzle over the dressing and serve immediately.

A platter de fruits de mer is one of the most delightful of all seafood experiences. Use this recipe as a guideline and choose whatever shellfish you find on the day.

Platter *of* Fruits *de* Mer

1 To prepare the seafood, steam the mussels, clams and cockles (if using) with just the water that clings to their shells, for 3–4 minutes until just open. Drain and refresh under cold running water. If you prefer to serve the oysters lightly cooked, which makes them easier to open, scrub them and put them into a pan with just a splash of water. Cook over a high heat for 3–4 minutes, drain and refresh under cold running water. Winkles and whelks need to be boiled in lightly salted water – winkles should be drained as soon as the water returns to a boil and whelks should be simmered for 4 minutes, then drained. Scallops should be steamed on the half shell until the flesh just turns white. Sea urchins need to be cut in half and drained of excess water.

2 To make the mayonnaise, put the egg yolk, mustard, lemon juice and seasoning into a food processor and process for 30 seconds until foaming. Gradually add the olive oil, drop by drop, until the mixture begins to thicken. Continue adding the oil in a steady stream until all the oil is incorporated. Season to taste with salt and pepper, if necessary, and add a little hot water if the mixture seems too thick. Leave to chill until required.

3 To make the shallot vinaigrette, mix the vinegar, shallots, oil and seasoning together. Leave to stand at room temperature for 2 hours.

4 To assemble the platter, place the seaweed on a large tray or platter and top with the crushed ice. Arrange the shellfish and crustaceans with the lemon wedges around the platter, scattering on more crushed ice as you go. Serve the mayonnaise and shallot vinaigrette separately.

SERVES 6

36 live mussels, scrubbed and bearded
18 live oysters
3 cooked lobsters, about 450 g/1 lb each
3 cooked crabs, about 750 g/1 lb 10 oz each
36 cooked langoustines or prawns
selection of clams, winkles, whelks
cockles, scallops and sea urchins
salt and pepper

mayonnaise
1 egg yolk
1 tsp Dijon mustard
1 tbsp lemon juice
300 ml/10 fl oz olive oil

shallot vinaigrette
150 ml/5 fl oz good-quality red wine vinegar
3 shallots, chopped finely
1 tbsp olive oil

to serve
seaweed
crushed ice
3 lemons, cut into wedges

NUTRITION
Calories *681*; Sugars *1 g*; Protein *41 g*;
Carbohydrate *3 g*; Fat *56 g*; Saturates *8 g*

 easy

2 hrs 20 mins

10–15 mins

As with many traditional French fish stews and soups, the fish and soup are served separately with a strongly flavoured sauce passed around to accompany them.

Bouillabaisse

SERVES 6 – 8

5 tbsp olive oil
2 large onions, chopped finely
1 leek, chopped finely
4 garlic cloves, crushed
½ small fennel bulb, chopped finely
5 ripe tomatoes, peeled and chopped
1 fresh thyme sprig
2 strips of orange rind
1.7 litres/3 pints hot fish stock
2 kg/4 lb 8 oz mixed fish, such as John Dory, sea bass, bream, red mullet, cod, skate, chopped roughly; soft shell crabs, raw prawns, langoustines (shellfish left whole)
12–18 thick slices French bread
salt and pepper

pepper and saffron sauce

1 red pepper, deseeded and quartered
150 ml/5 fl oz light olive oil
1 egg yolk
large pinch of saffron threads
pinch of crushed chillies
lemon juice, to taste

NUTRITION

Calories *844*; Sugars *10 g*; Protein *69 g*;
Carbohydrate *49 g*; Fat *43 g*; Saturates *6 g*

moderate

45 mins

45 mins

1 To make the red pepper and saffron sauce, brush the red pepper quarters with a little of the olive oil. Place under a preheated hot grill and, cook for about 5–6 minutes on each side until the skin is charred and blistered and the flesh is tender. Place the pepper in a polythene bag until cool enough to handle, then peel off the skins.

2 Place the pepper into a food processor with the egg yolk, saffron, crushed chillies, lemon juice and salt and pepper to taste and process until smooth. Gradually add the remaining olive oil, drop by drop, until the mixture begins to thicken. Continue adding the oil in a steady stream until all the oil is incorporated and the mixture is thick. Add a little hot water if it is too thick.

3 Heat the olive oil in a large saucepan over a low heat. Add the onions, leek, garlic and fennel and cook for 10–15 minutes until softened and beginning to colour. Add the tomatoes, thyme, orange rind and salt and pepper to taste and fry for a further 5 minutes until the tomatoes have collapsed.

4 Add the fish stock and bring to the boil over a medium heat. Simmer gently for 10 minutes until all the vegetables are tender. Add the fish and return to the boil. Simmer gently for 10 minutes until all the fish is tender.

5 When the soup is ready, toast the bread on both sides, then divide the fish between serving bowls. Add some of the soup to moisten the stew and serve with the toast. Serve the sauce and remaining soup separately.

Soufflés are always impressive and this one is no exception. Serve straight from the oven but don't worry if it sinks en route to the table – it's the nature of the beast.

Crab Soufflé

1 Generously grease a 1.4-litre/2½-pint soufflé dish. Add the breadcrumbs and shake around the dish to coat completely, shaking out any excess. Reserve on a baking sheet.

2 Melt the butter in a large saucepan over a low heat. Add the onion and cook gently for 8 minutes until softened, but not coloured. Add the garlic and cook for a further 1 minute. Add the mustard powder and flour and cook for 1 minute. Gradually add the milk, stirring until smooth. Increase the heat slightly and bring to the boil, stirring constantly. Simmer for 2 minutes. Remove from the heat and stir in the cheese. Leave to cool slightly.

3 Lightly beat in the egg yolks, then fold in the crab meat, chives, cayenne and season generously with salt and pepper.

4 Whisk the egg whites in a clean bowl until stiff peaks form. Add a large spoonful of the egg whites to the crab mixture and fold together to slacken. Add the remaining egg whites and fold together carefully, but thoroughly. Spoon into the prepared dish.

5 Cook in a preheated oven, 200°C/400°F/Gas Mark 6, for 25 minutes until well risen and golden. Serve immediately.

 COOK'S TIP

Place a baking sheet in the oven to preheat before cooking the soufflé. This helps keep the soufflé to rise.

SERVES 4 – 6

40 g/1½ oz butter, plus 1 tbsp for greasing
25 g/1 oz dried breadcrumbs
1 small onion, chopped finely
1 garlic clove, crushed
2 tsp mustard powder
25 g/1 oz plain flour
225 ml/8 fl oz milk
50 g/1¾ oz Gruyère cheese, grated
3 eggs, separated
225 g/8 oz fresh crab meat, thawed if frozen
2 tbsp snipped fresh chives
pinch of cayenne pepper
salt and pepper

NUTRITION

Calories 214; Sugars 1 g; Protein 15 g;
Carbohydrate 8 g; Fat 14 g; Saturates 7 g

 moderate

15 mins

35 mins

This is excellent served with the Quick Tomato Sauce that accompanies the Tuna Fish Cakes on page 103.

Spinach Roulade

SERVES 4

225 g/8 oz frozen spinach, thawed and well drained
25 g/1 oz/ butter, plus extra for greasing
25 g/1 oz plain flour
200 ml/7 fl oz milk
4 eggs, separated
1 tbsp chopped fresh tarragon
½ tsp freshly grated nutmeg
1 tbsp olive oil, for brushing
salt and pepper

filling

375 g/12 oz skinless smoked cod fillet
125 g/4 oz ricotta cheese
25 g/1 oz freshly grated Parmesan cheese
4 spring onions, chopped finely
2 tbsp freshly snipped chives
50 g/1¾ oz sun-dried tomatoes in olive oil, drained and finely chopped

NUTRITION
Calories *331*; Sugars *5 g*; Protein *27 g*;
Carbohydrate *10 g*; Fat *21 g*; Saturates *9 g*

✪✪✪   moderate

🕐   25 mins

🕐   40 mins

1 Grease a 33 x 23-cm/13 x 9-inch Swiss roll tin and line with baking paper. Squeeze the spinach to remove as much water as possible, then chop finely and reserve.

2 Melt the butter in a saucepan over a low heat. Add the flour and cook for about 30 seconds, stirring. Gradually add the milk, stirring constantly, until smooth. Bring slowly to the boil and simmer for 2 minutes, stirring. Remove from the heat and leave to cool slightly.

3 Stir in the spinach, egg yolks, tarragon, nutmeg and salt and pepper to taste. Whisk the egg whites until stiff peaks form. Fold a large spoonful into the spinach mixture to slacken it, then fold in the remaining egg whites, thoroughly but carefully, to avoid losing any volume. Pour the mixture into the prepared tin and smooth the surface.

4 Cook in a preheated oven, 200°C/400°F/Gas Mark 6, for 15 minutes until risen and golden and firm in the centre. Turn out immediately on to a clean tea towel, peel off the baking paper and roll up from one short end.

5 To make the filling, cover the fillet with boiling water and leave for about 10 minutes until just tender. Remove the fish and flake carefully, removing any bones, and mix with the ricotta, Parmesan cheese, spring onions, chives, sun-dried tomatoes and salt and pepper to taste.

6 Unroll the roulade and spread with the cod, leaving a 2.5-cm/1-inch border all around. Re-roll and return to the oven, seam side down, for 20 minutes.

This is definitely a fish pie for pushing out the boat! Serve piping hot with boiled new potatoes and a selection of freshly cooked vegetables.

Luxury Fish Pie

1 To make the filling, melt 25 g/1 oz of the butter in a frying pan over a medium heat. Add the shallots and cook for 5 minutes until softened. Add the mushrooms and cook for 2 minutes. Add the wine and cook until the liquid has evaporated. Transfer to a 1.5-litre/2¾-pint shallow ovenproof dish and reserve.

2 Put the mussels into a large pan with just the water that clings to their shells and cook, covered, over a high heat for 3–4 minutes until the mussels have opened. Discard any that remain closed. Strain, reserving the cooking liquid. Remove the mussels from their shells and add to the mushrooms.

3 Bring the court-bouillon to the boil over a low heat. Add the monkfish and poach for 2 minutes before adding the cod, sole and prawns. Poach for a further 2 minutes. Remove the fish with a slotted spoon and add to the mussels and mushrooms.

4 Melt the remaining butter in a saucepan over a low heat. Add the flour and stir until smooth. Cook for 2 minutes without colouring. Gradually, stir in the hot court-bouillon and mussel cooking liquid until smooth and thickened. Add the cream and simmer gently for 15 minutes, stirring. Season to taste with salt and pepper and pour over the fish.

5 Make the topping. Boil the potatoes in salted water for 15–20 minutes until tender. Drain and mash with the butter, egg yolks, milk, nutmeg and seasoning. Pipe over the fish and roughen the surface with a fork. Bake the pie in a preheated oven, 200°C/400°F/Gas Mark 6, for 30 minutes until golden and bubbling. Serve hot, garnished with parsley.

SERVES 4

85 g/3 oz butter
3 shallots, chopped finely
115 g/4 oz button mushrooms, halved
2 tbsp dry white wine
900 g/2 lb live mussels, scrubbed
   and bearded
1 x quantity Court-Bouillon (see page 150)
300 g/10½ oz monkfish fillet, cubed
300 g/10½ oz skinless cod fillet, cubed
300 g/10½ oz skinless lemon sole fillet, cubed
115 g/4 oz raw tiger prawns, peeled
25 g/1 oz plain flour
50 ml/2 fl oz double cream

potato topping
1.5 kg/3 lb 5 oz floury potatoes, peeled and cut
   into chunks
50 g/1¾ oz butter
2 egg yolks
125 ml/4 fl oz milk
pinch of freshly grated nutmeg
salt and pepper
fresh parsley sprigs, to garnish

NUTRITION
Calories *863*; Sugars *5 g*; Protein *66 g*;
Carbohydrate *60 g*; Fat *41 g*; Saturates *24 g*

 moderate
 10 mins
🕐 1 hr 10 mins

This is a really delicious and filling dish. Layers of potato slices and mixed fish are cooked in a creamy sauce and topped with grated cheese.

Layered Fish *and* Potato Pie

SERVES 4

900 g/2 lb waxy potatoes, peeled and sliced
5 tbsp butter
1 red onion, halved and sliced
5 tbsp plain flour
450 ml/16 fl oz milk
150 ml/5 fl oz double cream
225 g/8 oz smoked haddock fillet, cubed
225 g/8 oz cod fillet, cubed
1 red pepper, deseeded and diced
115 g/4 oz broccoli florets
55 g/2 oz freshly grated Parmesan cheese
salt and pepper

1 Bring a large saucepan of lightly salted water to the boil over a medium heat. Add the sliced potatoes and cook for 10 minutes. Drain and reserve.

2 Meanwhile, melt the butter in a saucepan over a low heat. Add the onion and fry gently for 3–4 minutes.

3 Add the flour and cook, stirring, for 1 minute. Blend in the milk and cream and bring to the boil, stirring, until the sauce has thickened.

4 Arrange half of the potato slices in the base of a shallow ovenproof dish.

5 Add the fish, red pepper and broccoli to the sauce and cook over a low heat for about 10 minutes. Season to taste with salt and pepper, then spoon the mixture over the potatoes in the dish.

6 Arrange the remaining potato slices in a layer over the fish mixture and then sprinkle the grated Parmesan cheese over the top.

7 Cook in a preheated oven, 180°C/350°F/Gas Mark 4, for 30 minutes or until the potatoes are cooked and the topping is golden.

NUTRITION
Calories 116; Sugars 1.9 g; Protein 6.2 g; Carbohydrate 9.7 g; Fat 6.1 g; Saturates 3.8 g

easy

10 mins

55 mins

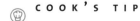 **COOK'S TIP**

Vary the fish used according to personal preference and availability. Do use fillets and remove as many of the bones as possible.

This fish pie is simplicity itself and can be prepared ahead and reheated just before serving.

Salmon *and* Courgette Pie

1 Heat the olive oil in a saucepan over a low heat. Add the peppers, onion and a little salt and pepper and cook gently for 10–15 minute, until softened. Transfer to a food processor or blender and process until smooth. Alternatively, rub through a fine sieve.

2 Bring a small saucepan of water to the boil over a medium heat. Add the eggs and cook for 10 minutes from when the water returns to the boil, then refresh immediately under cold running water. When cool enough to handle, drain and shell. Roughly chop the eggs and add to the pepper purée with the salmon, courgette, dill and seasoning. Mix well and reserve.

3 To make the pastry, put the flour into a bowl with the salt. Add the butter and rub it in with your fingertips until the mixture resembles fine breadcrumbs. Add the egg yolks with enough cold water to make a firm dough. Knead the dough on a lightly floured work surface until smooth.

4 Roll out a little over half of the dough and use to line a 23-cm/9-inch pie plate. Fill with the salmon mixture and dampen the edges with a little water. Roll out the remaining pastry and use to cover the pie, pinching the edges to seal. Make a cross or slash in the top of the pie for steam to escape. Re-roll any pastry trimmings, cut into fish tails or leaf shapes and use to decorate the edges of the pie, attaching them with a little beaten egg or milk. Brush more egg or milk over the rest of the pie to glaze.

5 Bake in a preheated oven, 200°C/400°F/Gas Mark 6, for 35–40 minutes until the pastry is golden. Garnish with Chinese garlic and serve.

SERVES 4

2 tbsp olive oil
2 red peppers, deseeded and chopped
1 onion, chopped finely
2 eggs
225 g/8 oz salmon fillet, skinned and cubed
1 courgette, sliced
1 tsp chopped fresh dill
salt and pepper
Chinese garlic, to garnish

pastry
350 g/12 oz plain flour, plus extra for dusting
½ tsp salt
175 g/6 oz cold butter, diced
2 egg yolks
3–4 tbsp cold water
beaten egg or milk, to glaze

NUTRITION
Calories *902*; Sugars *9 g*; Protein *28 g*;
Carbohydrate *77 g*; Fat *56 g*; Saturates *28 g*

 moderate

 40 mins

1 hr 10 mins

Hot-smoked trout is available from fishmongers and large supermarkets. The fish is smoked in a hot environment, which cooks the flesh as well as flavouring it.

Hot-smoked Trout Tart

SERVES 4

175 g/6 oz plain flour, plus extra for dusting
1 tsp salt
80 g/3 oz butter, cut into small pieces
1 egg yolk
2–3 tbsp cold water

filling

25 g/1 oz butter
1 small onion, chopped finely
1 tsp green peppercorns in brine, drained
   and roughly chopped
2 tsp stem ginger, drained
2 tsp stem ginger syrup
225 g/8 oz hot-smoked trout fillets, flaked
3 egg yolks
100 ml/3 1/2 fl oz crème fraîche
100 ml/3 1/2 fl oz double cream
1 tbsp chopped fresh parsley
1 tbsp snipped fresh chives
salt and pepper
lemon slices, to garnish
mixed salad leaves, to serve

NUTRITION

Calories *650*; Sugars *6 g*; Protein *22 g*;
Carbohydrate *40 g*; Fat *46 g*; Saturates *27 g*

 moderate

 1 hr

1 hr 20 mins

1 Sift the flour and salt together into a large bowl. Add the butter and rub it in with your fingertips until the mixture resembles coarse breadcrumbs. Add the egg yolk and enough cold water to form a firm dough. Knead briefly, wrap in clingfilm and leave to chill in the refrigerator for 30 minutes.

2 Meanwhile, make the filling. Melt the butter in a frying pan over alow heat. Add the onion and cook gently for 8–10 minutes until softened, but not coloured. Remove from the heat and stir in the peppercorns, ginger, ginger syrup and flaked trout. Reserve.

3 Remove the pastry from the refrigerator and roll out thinly on a lightly floured work surface. Use to line a 23-cm/9-inch flan tin or dish. Prick the base at regular intervals with a fork. Line the pastry with foil or baking paper and baking beans and bake in a preheated oven. 200°C/400°F/Gas Mark 6, for 12 minutes. Remove the foil or baking paper and beans and bake for a further 10 minutes until light golden and dry. Remove from the oven and leave to cool slightly. Reduce the oven temperature to 180°C/350°F/Gas Mark 4. Spread the trout mixture over the base of the pastry.

4 Mix the egg yolks, crème fraîche, cream, parsley, chives and seasoning together, then pour over the trout mixture to cover. Bake in the preheated oven for 35–40 minutes until just set and golden. Remove from the oven and leave to cool slightly. Transfer to 4 large serving plates, garnish with lemon slices and serve with mixed salad leaves.

Smoked haddock gives this tart a deliciously savoury flavour. Serve with a salad if wished.

Smoked Haddock *and* Spinach Tart

1 To make the pastry, mix both flours together in a bowl with the salt. Add the butter and rub it in with your fingertips until the mixture resembles fine breadcrumbs. Stir in enough cold water to form a firm dough. Knead the pastry briefly until the surface is smooth.

2 Roll out the dough thinly on a lightly floured work surface and use to line a 20-cm/8-inch deep fluted flan tin. Put the lined tin in the freezer for 15 minutes. Line with foil or baking paper and baking beans and place in a preheated oven, 200°C/400°F/Gas Mark 6, for 10–12 minutes. Remove the foil or paper and beans and bake for a further 10 minutes until pale golden and dry. Cool slightly. Reduce the oven temperature to 190°C/375°F/Gas Mark 5.

3 To make the filling, place the haddock in a frying pan, cover with milk and cream and bring to the boil over a medium–low heat. Cover and remove from the heat. Leave to stand for 10 minutes until the haddock is tender. Remove the fish with a slotted spoon. Strain the cooking liquid into a jug. Skin and flake the fish.

4 Press the spinach in a sieve or squeeze well to remove excess liquid. Arrange the spinach in the pastry case with the flaked fish. Add the egg yolks to the fish poaching liquid, together with 55 g/2 oz of the cheese and salt and pepper to taste. Mix and pour into the pastry case. Sprinkle over the remaining cheese and bake in the preheated oven for 25–30 minutes until the filling is risen, golden and just set. Cool briefly and serve with chicory.

SERVES 6

85 g/3 oz wholemeal flour, plus extra for dusting
85 g/3 oz plain flour
pinch of salt
85 g/3 oz chilled butter, diced
2–3 tbsp cold water

filling

350 g/12 oz smoked haddock fillet
150 ml/5 fl oz milk
150 ml/5 fl oz double cream
115 g/4 oz frozen leaf spinach, thawed
3 egg yolks, beaten lightly
80 g/3 oz mature Cheddar cheese, grated
salt and pepper
chicory, to serve

NUTRITION
Calories *458*; Sugars *3 g*; Protein *23 g*; Carbohydrate *21 g*; Fat *32 g*; Saturates *19 g*

★★★   moderate
    45 mins
    1 hr 10 mins

Index